Emerging Trends in Real Estate® Asia Pacific

2009

Contents

Editorial Leadership Team

Emerging Trends in Real Estate® Asia Pacific 2009 Chairs
Richard M. Rosan, Urban Land Institute
Robert K. Ruggles III, PricewaterhouseCoopers

Principal Authors and Senior Advisers
Colin Galloway, Urban Land Institute Consultant
Steven Laposa, PricewaterhouseCoopers

Senior Advisers and Contributing Researchers
Stephen Blank, Urban Land Institute
Chuck DiRocco, Urban Land Institue
Dean Schwanke, Urban Land Institute

Senior Adviser and Publisher
Rachelle L. Levitt, Urban Land Institute

PricewaterhouseCoopers Advisers and Contributing Researchers

Australia	James Dunning
	Brian Lawrence
China/Hong Kong	Gary Chan
	Alan Ho
	Peter E. Nieboer
	K.K. So
	Jacqueline S.Y. Wong
India	Deepak Dhanak
	Gautam Mehra
Japan	Raymond A. Kahn
	Hiroshi Takagi
Korea	Hyung-Ju Choi
	Jae-Dok Lee
	Jin-Young Lee
	Taejin Park
	YongJoon Yoon
Philippines	Malou P. Lim
Singapore	David Sandison
	Wee Hwee Teo

ULI Editorial and Production Staff
Nancy H. Stewart, Managing Editor
David James Rose, Manuscript Editor
Byron Holly, Senior Graphic Designer
Craig Chapman, Director of Publishing Operations
Karrie Underwood, Administrative Assistant

Recommended bibliographic listing:
ULI–the Urban Land Institute and PricewaterhouseCoopers LLP. *Emerging Trends in Real Estate® Asia Pacific 2009*. Washington, D.C.: ULI–the Urban Land Institute, 2008.

ULI Catalog Number: E36
ISBN: 978-0-87420-104-8

Executive Summary

Asia Pacific real estate markets have remained largely unscathed from direct damage related to the subprime implosion and subsequent credit crisis in the West, due largely to the absence of the type of structured credit instruments that led to the huge losses seen in U.S. markets. Asian banks' losses resulting from investment in derivatives listed on U.S. exchanges were minimal. Meanwhile, the only Asian country issuing statistically significant quantities of commercial mortgage–backed securities was Japan, and much of that market was dominated by international banks anyway. As a result, Asian banking systems remain for the most part well capitalized.

Likewise, yields have not been significantly affected by the turmoil. However, markets in several countries—in particular Japan, China, and India—have been subject to bank lending squeezes that began in 2007 as governments in those nations acted to combat overheated conditions in their domestic real estate sectors. Developers in those countries have borne the brunt of these measures, with many large builders forced into bankruptcy or experiencing severe shortages of capital.

Nonetheless, the continent will not escape the fallout. Regional stock markets have plummeted in 2008, with declines exaggerated as international investors repatriate their funds. Despite plenty of liquidity, banks have stopped lending to all but their best and biggest clients. Both debt and credit are therefore at best very difficult to find and then only at high prices. As a result, transaction turnover has ground to a halt, with few deals of note being done.

Banks have not been quick to call in loans, and many developers and investors have borrowed under terms that do not require financing until 2009 or 2010. There have therefore been few distress sales so far (although this is starting to change in China), and pricing had only begun to soften in most markets by the end of the year. However, the moment of truth will arrive when deals come up for refinancing. At this point, it is likely that many developers and investors will be unable to secure new funding on the right terms and will be forced to find a buyer. At this point, prices seem sure to turn south, although the extent of the downturn is hard to assess.

The likelihood that an economically strong Asia will be able to prop up the global economy as it enters recession is misguided. Despite growing consumer spending, Asian economies have yet to "decouple" from their reliance on exports to rich foreign countries, and as Western consumers consume less, the impact in Asia will be substantial. China, in particular, appears on the brink of a significant downturn.

There is currently a large exodus of foreign capital from Asia as Western investors continue to deleverage and cut risk. This is likely to turn the overall balance of capital flows to and from the region negative over the short term. However, opportunistic flows to regional real estate markets remain strong and many core investors looking for property assets are also rebalancing portfolios to take advantage of the (relatively) better economic prospects on offer across the continent. There is therefore likely to be plenty of investment capital available for real estate deals despite the downturn.

Both debt and credit will remain hard to come by, however. Where banks are willing to lend, leverage is reduced to 55 to 65 percent, down from previous levels of 80 to 90 percent. CMBS is dead everywhere except Japan, where one or two deals have gone through and the market seems deep enough to require a long-term securitization channel. In the future, deals will be done increasingly on local terms, however, which means they will be hard to arrange. Meanwhile, the shine has come off the local REIT industry, with almost all trading well below NAV at the end of 2008. While REIT prices are now so low they offer attractive yields, the large number of real estate investors now operating in Asia provides plenty of opportunity to exit deals, meaning the role previously played by REITs is not as pressing as before.

Based on investment prospect ratings, the top five markets in 2009 are Tokyo, Singapore, Hong Kong, Bangalore, and Shanghai. Four of the five cities from the previous year remain in the top five, with Bangalore being the addition jumping eight spots from 2008. Other cities with notable increases in rank include Mumbai, Taipei, and New Delhi. The top three cities with development opportunities were Bangalore, Ho Chi Minh City, and Mumbai.

In 2009, the office property sector tops the list of investment and development prospects, followed by the industrial/distribution sector. The hotel sector witnesses a major drop from first last year, due mostly to the slowing global economy. Overall, both industrial and development rating values were down for all property sectors compared to the previous year.

Preface

A joint undertaking of the Urban Land Institute (ULI) and PricewaterhouseCoopers, *Emerging Trends in Real Estate® Asia Pacific* is a trends and forecast publication now in its third year. The report provides an outlook on Asia Pacific real estate investment and development trends, real estate finance and capital markets, property sectors, metropolitan areas, and other real estate issues.

Emerging Trends in Real Estate® Asia Pacific 2009 represents a consensus outlook for the future and reflects the views of more than 180 individuals who completed surveys and/or were interviewed as a part of the research process for this report. Interviewees and survey participants represent a wide range of industry experts—investors, developers, property companies, lenders, brokers, and consultants. ULI and PricewaterhouseCoopers researchers personally interviewed over 60 individuals, and survey responses were received from more than 120 people whose company affiliations are broken down as follows:

Real Estate Service Firm	25.7%
Institutional/Equity Investor or Investment Manager	21.8%
Private Property Company or Developer	18.8%
Other Entity	15.8%
Publicly Listed Property Company or REIT	10.9%
Bank, Lender, or Securitized Lender	6.9%
Homebuilder or Residential Land Developer	0.0%

A list of the interview participants in this year's study appears at the end of this report. To all who helped, the Urban Land Institute and PricewaterhouseCoopers extend sincere thanks for sharing valuable time and expertise. Without the involvement of these many individuals, this report would not have been possible.

CHAPTER 1

The Calm Before the Storm

"The eternal optimist in me wants to see this as an anomaly that will pass shortly."

Amid the storm that swept through the world's financial markets in 2008, Asia's property sector remained an oasis of relative tranquility as it moved into the final quarter of the year. Economic conditions remained relatively strong. The banking sector appeared immune to subprime contagion. Real estate transactions had slowed to a trickle during the second half, but fundamentals and prices remained surprisingly strong, even as yields inched out as shifting perceptions of risk began to be priced into new deals.

But the calm is unlikely to last. During the first few weeks of September, the consensus among interviewees was that the financial crisis was a story of excess in Western economies and would play out mainly in Western markets. Local property markets would be supported by ongoing regional growth, a demographic favoring continuing urbanization, and a lack of direct exposure to subprime debt and toxic derivatives. But as the situation on Wall Street rapidly deteriorated later that month and into October, the mood in Asia darkened appreciably. And once it became clear that the consequences of Western excess included a virtual shutdown of the world's market for debt and, ultimately, a global recession, sentiment plunged. As one investor put it, "The eternal optimist in me wants to see this as an anomaly that will pass shortly, or at least one that won't [affect] the Asia Pacific [region] the same way it will the U.S. and western Europe, but my enthusiasm has waned."

Given the financial sector deleveraging still underway in global markets and the multitude of cross currents now in play, divining the implications for Asia's property sector is tricky. Markets are held hostage to a combination of fickle

EXHIBIT 1-1
Survey Responses by Country

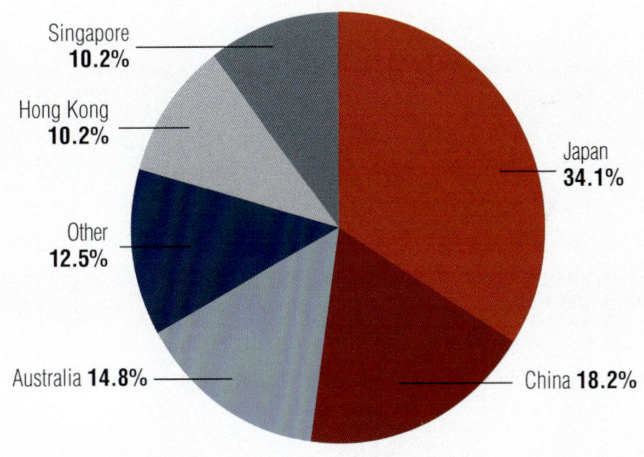

Source: *Emerging Trends in Real Estate Asia Pacific 2009* survey.

influences: the macroeconomy, capital flows, stock market fluctuations, government policy decisions, the health of the banking sector, and, most importantly, the impact of sentiment, be it consumer, bank, investor, or legislative. In the murk, however, a few things are evident. The full impact of the crisis may have occurred late in Asia (with the exception of the capital markets), but the day of reckoning is just around the corner. So, while the economic fallout may not hit the region as hard as it has in the West, at a minimum

EXHIBIT 1-2

Real Estate Transparency Scores: Asia Pacific

Tranparency Level	Country	2008 Rank*	2008 Score*	2006 Score
High Transparency	Australia	1	1.15	1.19
	New Zealand	4	1.25	1.19
	Hong Kong	9	1.46	1.50
	Singapore	9	1.46	1.55
Transparent	Malaysia	23	2.21	2.30
	Japan	25	2.40	3.08
Semitransparency	Taiwan	40	3.12	3.10
	South Korea	43	3.16	3.36
	Thailand	46	3.21	3.40
	Philippines	48	3.32	3.43
	China (First-Tier Cities)	49	3.34	3.71
	India (First-Tier Cities)	50	3.44	3.90
Low Transparency	Indonesia	55	3.59	4.11
	Vietnam	77	4.36	4.60

Source: Jones Lang LaSalle.

* All data as of July 2008.

Asia seems set to endure a round of falling asset prices and widening cap rates.

What's more, and perhaps more importantly, the investing landscape has undergone a substantive and possibly permanent change. Banks have rerated real estate for risk, and with the repricing of debt, investors will demand higher yields. The days of financing property (and most other) purchases via highly leveraged borrowing now appear to be gone, partly because lenders will not sanction it, and partly because the model itself has now been discredited. And with them, presumably, go the type of highly speculative private equity investors whose participation has contributed to the escalation of asset prices over recent years. All of which raises the question: Is downward pressure on property asset prices just part of the cycle, or is it a secular change?

Keeping It Simple

The apparent resilience of Asian economies in light of the financial woes in other parts of the world stems mainly from the fact that its markets have largely shunned the type of structured-credit products—mortgage-backed securities, collateralized debt obligations, credit default swaps—that led to such a disastrous descent in underwriting standards elsewhere.

In the West, banks lowered their risk assessment standards in order to feed investor appetite for the higher returns offered by bundled mortgages and other credit derivatives. The extra liquidity created by this easy credit gunned property prices and further compressed yields in bricks-and-mortar assets, which in turn had more investors drinking the securitization Kool-Aid. By contrast, most Asian property construction has remained financed by bank borrowing: "The banks are typically doing club deals—just going out and syndicating, selling down different tranches to different banks; syndicating is a lot easier because it doesn't involve rating agencies."

With relatively little use of mortgage-backed securities or other credit derivatives, and effectively no subprime lending, the banking sector has avoided the feedback loop that ultimately made the crash in Western markets a self-fulfilling prophecy. As a result, in late 2008 Asia's financial counters remain remarkably strong, with record profits ensuring ample liquidity and strong capital bases. While a handful of large banks in China, Japan, and Singapore have been hit with significant losses from investments in U.S. property derivatives, writedowns have been minimal as a proportion of deposit bases, and pose no threat to bank solvency.

On the other side of the coin are the regional housing markets. Although housing price rises over the last five years have been steep in most countries, the driver has not, as in the United States, been easy access to cheap credit. Excluding Japan, Asian buyers may be more inclined to speculate than in the West, but prices have generally been driven more by increasing incomes than easy credit. For example, according to Morgan Stanley economist Qing Wang, house prices in China have actually declined substantially relative to household income since 1997 because, even as real values have doubled and tripled, nominal household earnings have grown even faster. This method of measuring affordability is not without its critics (partly because the ratio of housing prices to income is far higher in China [at eight to nine times] than it is in the West [three to six times]). The point, however, is that house

EXHIBIT 1-3

Real Estate Firm Profitability Forecast

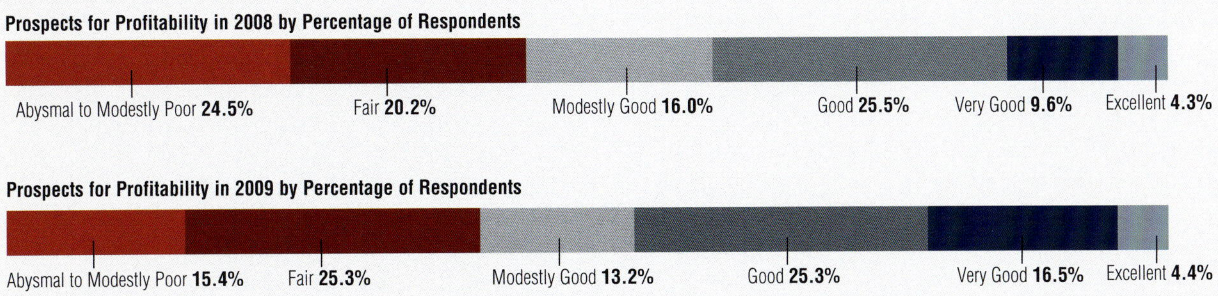

Source: *Emerging Trends in Real Estate Asia Pacific 2009* survey.

EXHIBIT 1-4

Historical Real Estate Firm Profitability Trends

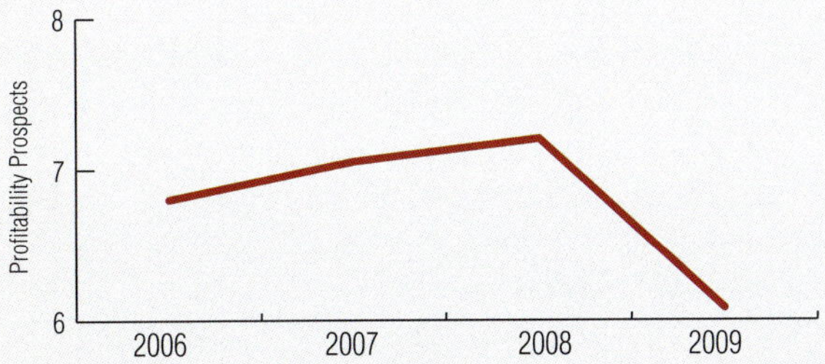

1 = Abysmal, 5 = Fair, 7 = Good, 9 = Excellent.

Source: *Emerging Trends in Real Estate Asia Pacific 2009* survey.

EXHIBIT 1-5

Change in Availability of Debt Capital for Real Estate by Source Type

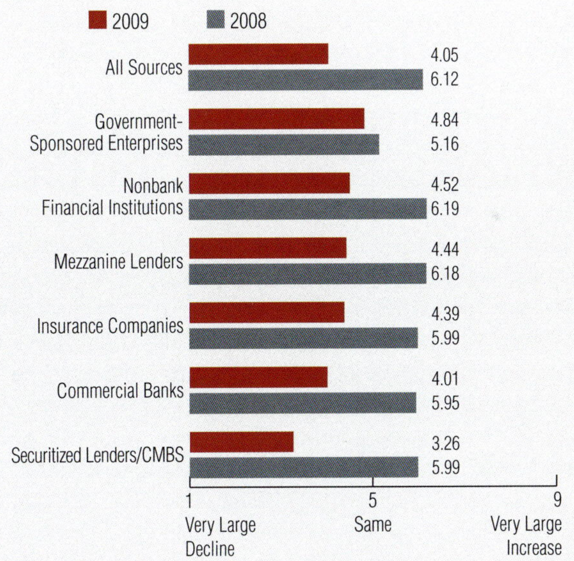

Source: *Emerging Trends in Real Estate Asia Pacific 2009* survey.

price inflation in the region has been driven by a separate mechanism than it was in the United States.

Both the banks and the residential property market have therefore effectively dodged the subprime bullet. This does not mean, of course, that they can dodge the ensuing fallout, but it may explain the relatively bullish sentiment reflected in our survey responses to profitability projections for 2009. Whether those expectations can be sustained in the post-meltdown reality, however, is another matter.

The Credit Freeze

Unsurprisingly, the number-one issue identified by interviewees was difficulty in getting credit. Asian banks may have had few problems so far with bad debts, but as paranoia spread through global financial markets in late 2008, local money markets froze up and Asian banks became as reluctant to lend as their Western peers. Banks scrambled to rerate risk, reduce exposure on their balance sheets, and assess viability of counterparties. Borrowers for commercial property deals have had an especially skeptical response. Not only are banks "rationing credit to commercial real estate because it's long-term lending," but real estate borrowers are deemed guilty by association with events that transpired in the West because banks fear that "contagion of lax lending standards" might start to appear in the commercial property sector. By the final quarter, debt had become "much harder to get as well as more expensive."

Emerging Trends survey responses provided in September, just prior to the October collapse, reflect significant contraction in debt availability from all sources compared to the previous year as seen in Exhibit 1-5. Since the survey was completed, the situation in the market has deteriorated, and the credit squeeze became a chokehold at the beginning of the fourth quarter, culminating in the near-paralysis of regional debt markets (see Chapter 2).

However, access to credit across the region varies considerably depending on both investor type and location. Larger, better-capitalized names with good track records can still get loans, albeit at a price "200 to 300 points more now than before." According to one fund manager, "It's very difficult to get debt at any cost. Having said that, for experienced market players, the banks will follow and you can still get very good terms." Says another: "I don't think the window is closed, but banks are being very careful about who they lend to; there's a bit of a return to relationship banking, even though spreads are going out."

Also, assets in some markets may prove easier to finance than in others. In Japan, for example, "There's very little debt available, but it depends on the asset. You want to buy a Tokyo office building or a well-located retail asset in central Tokyo? Ten different lenders will trip over themselves to give you a deal. Residential is a lot trickier."

In China, meanwhile, the landscape for borrowers is barren. As one interviewee observed, "Debt is virtually impossible to obtain even if you are a first-division player." That applies to foreigners as much as to locals. Overseas investors have been hit by a slew of government regulations introduced since 2006 that have sought to limit access for foreign real estate investors, who have come to be regarded by Beijing as a destabilizing influence for at least a couple of reasons. First, foreign players had begun to muscle domestic investors out of deals in the major cities, creating a wave of nationalistic hysteria. Second, the Chinese real estate sector had become a magnet for vast amounts of international "hot money" that sought to hitch a free ride on the gradual, government-controlled appreciation of the local currency against the U.S. dollar. Foreigners have faced special difficulty purchasing high-value finished assets (i.e., those over US$100 million). However, as the local market began to turn south in late 2008 (and as the hot-money flows began moving out of China), there were indications that these restrictions might be eased, especially in secondary locations. In any event, China remains "probably the market where, financially, life is toughest under the present scenario."

Refinancing: The Day of Reckoning?

It is one thing if a lack of credit simply stops deals from being done because investors can no longer leverage up. It has entirely more ominous implications, though, for existing borrowers and in particular for the legion of investors who for years have been paying top dollar for Asian assets in high-leverage, low-interest deals and who must now return to the well to refinance just as banks have slammed their doors shut. According to one fund manager, "The crunch will come when they have to roll the debt. If the values have fallen and the banks' appetite for high loan-to-value or mezzanine-type lending has diminished, their ability to refinance will be constrained." At that point, investors will be subject to foreclosure and forced sale. So far, the moment of truth has yet to arrive. "On a lot of the big projects, the developers are quite cashed up, they've had a couple of good years and they just say, 'I'm going to sit on it because I locked in this financing two years ago and it's costing me nothing to hold property.' "

The exception to this is in China and Japan, where the credit squeeze began earlier than in the rest of Asia. In Japan, Western investment banks withdrew from the market around the end of 2007, and with local banks unwilling to fill the void, the market became illiquid very rapidly. Dozens of Japanese developers have been forced into bankruptcy during 2008 as a direct result. As one investment banker active in Japan observed, "The defaults are coming from the fact that they can't refinance—it's not because the fundamentals are bad and people are moving out of buildings, or that rents are going down dramatically and they can't support the debt service."

In the early stages of the global credit crisis, commercial real estate has not been in the firing line. But excessive price rises and highly leveraged deal-making have not been confined to the residential sector and the current lack of credit "is like the third nail in the coffin." Going into the fourth quarter of 2008, nonresidential real estate markets globally were beginning to turn south for just this reason. The refinancing question therefore promises to become a huge issue in Asia (and elsewhere too) during 2009 and into 2010 as a multitude of short-term and construction loans mature. More than any other, this issue may prove to be the catalyst that finally brings the crisis home to regional real estate markets. Problems will be particularly acute for buyers who have pushed the financing envelope, predicating investments on unlikely yield projections and a presumption that values would continue to rise. Because many such deals related to sales of existing buildings, there are likely to be sales of completed projects as well as developments. Although the fallout is uncertain, there are probably many outstanding deals that will not be refinanced at any price. This raises the familiar prospect for 2009 and after of a downward spiral of developer bankruptcies, forced sales, and sinking prices. The flip side, of course, is that there is also the prospect of a multitude of projects coming to the market at fire-sale prices.

Asian Banks Not Rushing to Foreclose—Yet

One reason why so few distressed sales have occurred in Asia so far is that lenders have been reluctant to foreclose on existing borrowers. In an environment where banks generally remain well capitalized and bad debts have been thin on the ground, lenders have little incentive to force the issue. Given that mortgages are rarely securitized, local banks have more leeway to negotiate extensions than they would if the loan is packaged and dispatched internationally into the black hole of securitization. As one fund manager said: "Banks are being very accommodating because they know that if they start foreclosing on these rollovers, it's just going to force values to fall further. I suspect that while there's a belief out there that borrowers are able to service debt, the industry will try to carry debtors over the next year or two until the debt markets stabilize, because as soon as you start to see widespread defaults and fire sales, that tends to mean prices falling further—just look at the American residential market." In addition, authorities in some countries and in particular China have been slow to enforce regulations (such as project construction deadlines) that would create problems for cash-deprived developers.

According to one interviewee, the forbearance on debt rollover applies especially to the region's two biggest markets: "We've seen it in Australia definitely—banks have been more willing to let borrowers work out the situation, and I think that's also common in Japan." This has probably helped to stem the contagion in the region and is one reason why Asia has lagged the global decline in real estate markets, with property prices in most areas remaining relatively buoyant even as markets in the West have faded or collapsed. Whether banks continue to accommodate this approach as more and more loans come up for refinancing and as economic fundamentals in the region deteriorate is an open—but crucial—question, and one on which most interviewees had a negative take.

No-Deal-Making Desert

Unsurprisingly, in the current environment, transaction volumes have plummeted: "The market's gone into limbo"; "we are in a wait-and-see mode"; and "everyone's sitting on the sidelines waiting for the dust to settle," were some of the many comments we heard. According to Real Capital Analytics, Asian property sales in the third quarter plunged 68 percent year on year, compared with just 18 percent in the year through August, with Australia suffering the steepest decline of 74 percent, similar to declines experienced in the United States. Prospective sellers are hunkered down hoping for a miracle. Buyers, meanwhile, are either hamstrung by a lack of debt or biding their time waiting for lower prices. The lack of willing sellers means that competition for deals remains high (although it "may be less difficult than it was") even as large numbers of potential buyers have been taken out of the equation.

Another factor that may soon flush out more sellers is the "denominator effect." Where funds hold real estate as a weighted percentage of their portfolios and the proportion of property assets rises because the value of other fund assets (e.g., equities) has declined, funds are forced to sell property assets in order to rebalance. In this case, the denominator effect is caused essentially by the fact that Asian assets have outperformed those elsewhere in the world, creating the paradox that "Asia is being punished for overperformance." This applies mainly to core funds, which tend to have more rigid investment structures. Many are considering adjusting their numerators to allow them to continue to invest in Asian assets or even increase their previous allocation.

In China, where the music in real estate construction stopped in late 2007 following a wave of government-led regulatory measures, activity at government land auctions has halted, with land attracting few or no bids at prices far below those of the previous year. In fact, there are more developers trying to return land they bought at auctions in previous years than there are purchasing new land. This compares to the rabid competition witnessed in 2007, when developers lost discipline and began bidding crazy prices, sometimes paying more for an undeveloped site than they would be able to charge for finished properties built on it. In the southern city of Guangzhou, land auctions brought in about US$1.6 billion in the first half of 2008, according to local press reports, just a quarter the equivalent

EXHIBIT 1-6

Average Real Estate Yields in Average Markets

	Yield (%) Grade A Office (%)*	Prime Retail (%)*	Luxury Residential (%)*	Industrial (%)*
Bangkok	6.6–8.2	11.9–12.3	4.9–5.2	6.0–7.0
Beijing	7.8–9.8	6.8–8.8	5.5–7.5	9.0–10.0
Chengdu	9.5–12.0	7.5	NA	7.2
Delhi	11.5	11.0	2.0–3.0	10.0–12.0
Hanoi	NA	NA	NA	NA
Ho Chi Minh City	NA	NA	NA	NA
Hong Kong	4.1–6.6	4.1	3.0	6.9
Jakarta	8.0–8.2	15.0–15.5	10.8–11.2	8.5–10.3
Kuala Lumpur	7.15–7.35	7.0–10.0	7.5–8.0	NA
Macau	NA	5.9	3.3	NA
Makati (Philippines)	10.4–10.8	11.3–11.7	6.6–7.0	NA
Mumbai	11.4	10.9	3.5–5.0	NA
Seoul	5.5	NA	3.0–4.0	7.0–7.5
Singapore	5.8–6.3	5.3	2.8	4.7
Shanghai	7.3–8.9	11.1	5.1–7.2	8.0–9.0
Sydney	5.75–6.25	5.0–7.25	NA	7.8
Taipei	4.5	NA	NA	4.5–5.0
Tokyo	3.3	NA	4.8–5.5	4.8–5.3

Sources: Jones Lang LaSalle, CB Richard Ellis.

* Data as of June 30, 2008.

figure for the previous year. On the residential front, home sales by volume dived 55.5 percent in Beijing and 38.5 percent in Shanghai in the first eight months of 2008. In the investment market, however, the total investable value of major transactions (i.e., US$10 million–plus) soared 86 percent year on year to about US$25 billion in the first half of 2008, according to consultants DTZ, as more and more distressed developers began selling off half-finished product, with most sales taking place in secondary markets. Significantly, just 3 percent of these transactions by value involved foreign purchasers, reflecting how effectively government regulations are blocking outside investment in Chinese property deals. That said, both foreign funds and big Asian developers are awaiting their chance for the market to reopen. With fewer rules applying to buying stakes in ongoing projects as opposed to buying completed assets, this is a niche many foreign players are looking at.

In Australia, property fundamentals remain relatively strong, driven by the country's commodities boom. However, indebted real estate investment trusts (REITs) are busy trying to unload properties worth some US$12 billion as of October in an attempt to raise funds to cut borrowing, which has become prohibitively expensive as spreads have widened. Many international funds are said to be sniffing around looking for deals, and the logjam is expected to break soon.

Japan also is seeing pressure for transactions. According to another investor, "Because that was such a highly leveraged market, I think you'll probably see the cap rate widening in Japan first as opposed to southeast Asia, where a lot of the buyers didn't rely on leverage so much." And another: "The residential sector is where the illiquidity is, on the debt side. You have a lot of people who bought that stuff using short-term financing because they thought they could buy it, lease it up, and flip it. Now they bought it, leased it, and can't flip it. They have notes coming through, they can't get other financing, and the alternative basically is to sell it for what they can get."

Yields Still Holding Strong. . .

When the curtain came down on Western markets in the early months of 2008, many investors fled to Asia in the belief that local markets would be insulated from the maelstrom. As a result, average regional yields actually contracted in the first half to around 5.25 percent, according to RCA. As seen in Exhibit 1-6, third-quarter yields have begun to widen as the crisis has deepened and the economic situation has deteriorated. The problem is that with so little action in the market, widening yields are hard to make out. As one investor says, "In theory, yields have to have gone out even by 100 basis points, but I don't think that we can prove it yet because we don't have 50 examples of transactions this year versus 50 last year." Another, speaking in September, observed: "If you look around the region, yields have moved out between 50 and 100 basis points, and you could argue given what's going on, that's probably not enough. But that's an effect of the liquidity that's still about, and if there's anything of any quality, there's still fairly aggressive competition to acquire it."

The lack of movement in yields is also a consequence of the fact that the refinancing effect, as noted above, has yet to kick in, while throughout the region market fundamentals (demand/supply, occupancy rates, affordability ratios, etc.) have remained largely resilient, with signs of softening only beginning to appear in the fourth quarter.

Still, yields have started to move in some sectors and geographies. In Japan, "residential yields have clearly moved and probably are at historic highs upward of 6 to 7 percent or even anecdotally in regional cities closer to 9 percent." In China, residential prices have also dropped, though official figures have been slow to reflect it. There, the catalyst has been government measures aimed at slowing inflation and deterring speculators. According to one consultant, "Last year, we saw about 20 to 25 percent coming off [prices] in Shenzhen and Guangzhou, and maybe 12 to 15 percent in Shanghai. We've already seen in the first half [of 2008] probably half that again, and the anticipation is that what we saw last year will probably be repeated this."

One factor that has aggravated house price declines in China and elsewhere is that cash-strapped developers are resorting to preselling more units "just to keep the wheel turning." Some of the large Chinese developers "have people actually doubling their sales volume this year just to pay for ongoing construction." In an environment where buyers are already leery of market declines, the only way to shift product is to discount it. Presales are now beginning earlier and occurring in larger volumes.

In India, too, bank financing began to dry up in 2007 following a government clampdown, and debt is now available only at astronomical prices, with "behind the scenes, some developers borrowing money at anything around 3 percent per month." As a result, development companies have slashed prices to unload projects they cannot fund. According to one consultant, "Anybody who put money into Indian real estate one or two years ago has today seen the value being eroded."

. . . But Reversals a Question of When, Not If

Still, the consensus among most investors is that a substantial decline in pricing is baked into the new scenario. "We've started to see it, but we're going to see a lot more of it. There are a lot of developers out there who paid top dollar for land a few months ago who are now looking at the holding costs, redoing their feasibility numbers, and not coming up with pretty answers."

The question is: when to invest? Many interviewees proved to be trigger shy, citing the purchases (mainly in the financial sector) of some of the big sovereign fund investors early in 2008, which were deeply underwater just a few months later. According to one opportunistic fund manager, "The general sense is that this situation isn't over yet. I think everyone knows some deep-discounted deals are going to happen. But clearly there is still a sense where sellers expect they can get maybe a 5 or 10 percent discount compared to six months ago—I'm saying no, I want a 25 percent discount and maybe I'll consider it." Just when that moment arrives will probably depend largely on the term of the debt that needs to be refinanced. "A lot of the projects were started a couple of years ago and have four- to five-year financing, so we're probably 18 months away," said one fund manager.

In Japan, many bank loans are structured to become due at the end of the fiscal year in March. One investor recalled negotiating "huge discounts" in previous years where "there was a mad rush to do deals because sellers waited until the last minute and suddenly your ability to close the deal is more important than the price you pay. It'll be interesting to see if it goes back to these kinds of dynamics—I think it's likely."

One way in which Asian property may become cheaper by default is via currency depreciation, which has already made real estate in some jurisdictions considerably cheaper in U.S. dollar terms. The Australia dollar, for example, has sunk against the greenback in 2008, just as the domestic REIT industry has collapsed because of rising borrowing costs. By the beginning of the third quarter, some US$12 billion worth of commercial property assets were up for sale as listed property trusts (LPTs) seek to raise cash. Middle East investors and funds from Germany were reported to be in the market sniffing for deals.

Economics: The Myth of Decoupling

The prospect of a widespread economic retrenchment as the crisis spreads from the financial sector to the real economy is the issue that has interviewees most worried. So far, the resilience of Asia's emerging markets has cushioned the impact of the crash in Western economies. Excluding Japan, east Asia's nine largest economies grew about 8 percent year on year in the first half of 2008, compared with just 2.3 percent in the United States and 1.8 percent in the EU.

While economists have now lowered their growth estimates for 2009, many still expect Asia's economies will continue to man the barricades while the rest of the world sorts itself out.

Nonetheless, risk is still to the downside. One potentially major problem is that the credit freeze will cause economies to seize up. A lack of credit constrains deal flow, and may create a vicious circle of negative sentiment, deteriorating credit quality, and plunging asset values, both within the property sector and the economy generally. As one interviewee said, "The real estate industry thrives on transactions and the velocity of money, and as the banks hold back, [they are] cutting off the lifeblood. The concern for me is how does that affect the real economy? I'm not sure where that impact is going to hit or how hard, but that's the big risk for the entire industry."

In addition, even if Asian fundamentals remain sound, the region is not immune to the impact of a global recession, no matter how much some analysts insist that regional economies have outgrown their trade-based models. By the end of the third quarter of 2008, regional economies had begun to wilt, emerging and developed alike. Stock markets from India to Hong Kong had sunk 30 to 70 percent from last year's highs. Singapore was in recession. In Japan, growth turned negative in the second quarter and is expected to remain that way through 2009. Meanwhile, recent investment bank forecasts have further slashed growth projections. In October, Morgan Stanley twice cut 2009 gross domestic product (GDP) figures for ASEAN countries (from 5.1 percent to 3.6 percent).

The steady erosion of economic conditions across the region explodes the myth that Asia is now decoupled from the West's business cycles. Both the depth and the duration of the events stemming from the subprime collapse have created a negative feedback loop that brings the crisis to Asia's doorstep through trade and financial market connections. Western consumers are consuming fewer Asian exports, while the negative sentiment and credit paralysis created by the unwinding of toxic debt in the West have hammered local stock markets and paralyzed money market funding along with other types of debt. The key in such an environment will be to boost domestic demand, pump-priming local economies, mainly through infrastructure investment.

EXHIBIT 1-7

Asia Pacific Economic Growth: Consensus Forecasts

	Real GDP Growth Rate (%)					
	2009*	2008*	2007	2006	2005	2004
China	9.25	9.74	11.90	11.60	10.40	10.10
India	6.94	7.93	9.34	9.82	9.13	7.89
Singapore	3.45	3.62	7.72	8.17	7.30	8.99
Indonesia	5.51	6.08	6.32	5.51	5.69	5.03
Thailand	4.53	4.74	4.75	5.11	5.53	6.34
Malaysia	4.75	5.75	6.35	5.78	5.33	6.78
South Korea	3.49	4.12	4.97	5.13	4.20	4.73
Taiwan	2.50	3.83	5.72	4.89	4.16	6.15
Philippines	3.80	4.40	7.19	5.40	4.95	6.38
Hong Kong	3.47	4.09	6.37	7.02	7.08	8.47
Asia and Pacific	5.60	6.00	7.60	7.50	6.80	6.80
Australia	2.24	2.49	4.17	2.74	2.81	3.86
New Zealand	1.48	0.65	3.22	1.94	2.74	4.52
Japan	0.47	0.69	2.08	2.42	1.93	2.74

Sources: International Monetary Fund, Moody's.
* Projections.

Can China Save the World?

As usual, the joker in the pack will be China, which was the biggest contributor to global growth in 2007, according to the International Monetary Fund. As a big buyer of components, equipment, and raw materials from other parts of Asia, the Mainland has become an important engine for regional economies. As a rule of thumb, for every 1 percentage point of Chinese GDP growth, a half percentage point is added to Asia's developing economies (and vice versa). The importance of these links is reflected in the trade figures: some 35 percent of Taiwanese exports, 25 percent of South Korean exports, and 31 percent of the Philippines' exports are shipped to China. Hong Kong's economy also is heavily integrated with China. Australia, meanwhile, is highly dependent on the Mainland as a buyer of raw materials, from iron ore to coal, oil, and gas. Finally, with China overtaking the United States as its biggest trading partner in July, even Japan is now held hostage to Chinese consumption.

Ominously, however, China may not be able to deliver. Signs of a significant slowdown were unmistakable in late 2008. GDP growth dropped to 9 percent in the third quarter, significantly more than expected. Businesses have been hit by soaring costs for land, labor, and raw materials just as the government has tightened bank lending in an effort to cool inflation. Raw materials purchasing is falling. Manufacturing is contracting. Investment also is weakening, particularly in the property sector, which for various reasons acts as a lynchpin for investment in other areas (in particular infrastructure). And rumors are rife about small and medium-sized businesses going belly-up all over the country. Some analysts believe that China is now better equipped to handle external shocks because its newly enriched consumers will pick up the slack from declining exports. But the reality is that private consumption in China has always been weak and is unlikely to become a major economic driver anytime soon, not least because so many Chinese consumers have ploughed their savings into either the local stock market (which has tanked more than

70 percent in a year) or the residential property market, which is shaky to say the least. Trade, on the other hand, is economically more important than ever. U.S. imports of Chinese goods have risen from 2 percent of Chinese GDP during the last U.S. recession in 2001 to about 10 percent currently. Exports to Europe are even higher. This means that as Chinese exports fall in the wake of vanishing consumer demand in the West, the knock-on effect for the Chinese economy will be significant. Already, Chinese export growth has dropped precipitously (to 10.4 percent in September measured in local currency terms). Some economists are projecting negative export growth for 2009.

Beijing will be able to prime the economy by boosting infrastructure spending, as it has in the past. Fortunately, with about US$1.9 trillion in foreign reserves, it has plenty of capital to throw at the problem. But while this may help China and, by extension, other Asian countries to avoid the full force of the downturn now unfolding in the United States and Europe, doubt remains about the region's capacity to prop up global growth as expected. If Asia's ability to bail out the global economy proves to be exaggerated, the current downturn may be longer and deeper than expected.

Inflation

Over the last several years, China's insatiable appetite for raw materials, from iron ore to soy beans, has been the major driver of steep rises in global commodity prices. By early 2008, these inflationary pressures in Asia had built up to an alarming degree. In China, price rises peaked at 8.7 percent year on year in February, sparking fears that price pressures would erode corporate profits and jeopardize investment. In Indonesia, India, and the Philippines, the consumer price index (CPI) rose to the low double digits, while in Vietnam prices spiked to almost 30 percent in the third quarter, creating a major macro problem for the economy and making Vietnam property plays—the darling of Asian investors in 2007—"not overly compelling" today. So far, supply shortages have propped up prices for commercial property and softened the declines in the residential sector, but Vietnam has seen a sharp falloff in real estate starts.

More recently, pricing concerns have been obscured by more pressing economic issues. Although interest rates are in general likely to be kept low in an attempt to stimulate growth, inflation now seems an unlikely enemy in a recessionary environment, especially as demand for commodities from China and elsewhere has plummeted in the second half of 2008. Because China is by far the biggest contributor to net global demand growth for commodities across the board, Chinese demand is also the key driver of global commodities price movements. Prices for steel, iron ore, aluminum, copper, and a slew of other raw materials (including, to an extent, oil) have recently fallen dramatically as a result.

The powerful deflationary influence that has emerged from this is important for Asia's real estate investors not so much on a macro level, but because it eases a major problem that has been hurting regional developers quite apart from the credit squeeze. As one investor says, "Inflation has been hitting especially badly, so it's a double whammy. Not only have developers got to meet construction costs, but they have a larger construction bill, and in China today you're looking at construction costs rising 15 percent per annum—that's very hard to swallow and still make your margins."

Flight to Quality

In recent years, many investors who had been muscled out of deals in major Asian cities by core funds or high-leverage private equity players willing to accept compressed yields sought refuge in secondary locations or products in an effort to find value. And many were very successful in doing so, although risks were commensurately high. In today's environment, however, investors are again focusing on prime assets in major locations. With funding so hard to get, new construction in many prime areas has dropped. And because few markets in Asia suffer from overbuilding (with some notable exceptions, especially in parts of China and India), there is little overhang in property stock, which should help to put a floor under pricing at the top end. "In a down market, it makes a lot of sense to focus on quality," commented one opportunistic fund manager. "Over the last two years, Hong Kong, Singapore, Shanghai, Beijing, and Tokyo have all become ludicrously expensive and suitable only for core investors. But that's going to change as we see prices come off and yields go up—there will be opportunities for other people to play there again." As a result, investors at prime sites are more likely to recover their equity following a forced sale.

At the same time, projects in secondary markets or even in less well-positioned prime areas are more likely to run into problems, especially as slowing growth lowers demand for commercial premises. The problem is aggravated by the fact that good-quality office and retail property in Asia is thin on the ground. According to ING Real Estate, only Japan (at 16 percent of the global market) has particularly large volumes of investment-grade property. After that, South Korea (3 percent) and China (2 percent) offer few options. "A lot of what's built is really not top notch," said one investor. "And when recently you had lots of money chasing scant product there was very little differentiation between what was grade A and grade C, so that's where the fallout will be. Some of the foreign funds that have bought may have to make significant corrections in valuations where they bought something less than grade A."

Winners and Losers

In the new reality, there will be winners and losers. The losers come in several varieties. Foreign investment banks, where they are investing on their own behalf, have been sucked into the violent deleveraging process still underway on Wall Street. Not only have they stopped lending in Asia, but they may also be liquidating assets to send cash to their operations in other parts of the world. "We have problems," commented a real estate executive at one such bank. "We see new investment in the region coming not from the traditional investment banks anymore. Regardless of whether real estate is good or not, on Wall Street they say 'get rid of it.' Reduce balance sheets for real estate—I think that's fairly universal and it's going to be a theme going forward."

Hot money will be another victim. The market is going to spit out "anyone playing this super-leverage game where they're trying to put in $5 for a $100 project."

According to a risk management director at a large U.S.-owned fund, investors who could achieve 85 percent LTVs not long ago are now being restricted to 50 percent LTVs, "and then you're needing mezzanine funds to come in and pick up the gap and they're probably only willing to go up to maybe 65 percent LTV." This takes out "the hedge funds trying to get the 25 percent returns and the only way they can get there is by massive leverage."

Some large pension funds that may have suffered losses elsewhere are in the same boat. Add to the pot numerous small and not-so-small developers hit by the credit freeze, as well as a number of large corporations that may need to raise funds by striking sale and leaseback transactions, and you have a high number of potential distressed sellers, although at this point there is very little transparency as to how far the selling may extend.

With so many likely liquidations in the pipeline, "that's where you start talking about opportunistic possibilities." Predictably, the winners will be those with ready cash. That means, in particular, the large, locally based, heavily capitalized developers who operate across the region, especially from places like Singapore and Hong Kong. Some interviewees suggested they may be joined by the larger Japanese developers who retreated to their home turf during the last financial crisis in Asia during 1997 and have not been seen regionally since. While their share prices have been knocked way down, these companies are generally well capitalized and well connected, and will probably have little problem getting credit if they need it. Already, Hong Kong and Singapore developers have begun actively sifting possibilities in China, picking up land or distressed assets at bargain prices.

In addition, there are many opportunistic funds operating in Asia (both local and international) that are now waiting their chance, as well as "a stack of equity" coming to Asia from the West on the lookout either for distressed assets or in general for a more fertile investment environment than Western markets may be able to offer for several years. In fact, private equity funds brought a total of US$26.3 billion of new capital to Asia's emerging markets in the first half of 2008, almost half of it earmarked for China. That's more than double the figure from the same period in 2007, according to the Emerging Markets Private Equity Association. Just how these funds will fare, though, is a "wheels within wheels" question given that "they may need a reasonably high amount of leverage to get the returns that they are promising, while their prospects for raising finance must be questionable."

Green Buildings

Most interviewees acknowledge a gradual shift in perceptions toward greater use of sustainable construction practices, but the reality is that markets remain price sensitive before all else, and any real implementation tends to take place in only a few top-end properties. However, the attitude varies from place to place. In India, for example, government regulations mandate that real estate investments "of more than about $12 million must go to the central or state government for an environmental impact assessment," and the government is now working on creating green building norms that will have to be followed. According to one locally based consultant, "There are also a lot of private initiatives. I know many Indian developers that have a vision statement saying that every single one of their buildings from now on will either be a Platinum or Gold LEED-rated building." In Thailand, on the other hand, "outside some of the better-quality resorts, there are few projects that could claim to be green at the moment. It's probably a very low priority for the government, which is focused on dealing with a political crisis."

Finally, in China, where the sheer scale of ongoing construction and the generally poor track record of environmental protection make the issue perhaps more pressing than anywhere in Asia: "It's on the radar as a marketing angle. Chinese developers will claim to be environmentally friendly because they've put a solar panel on the roof, but it's still a bit of a tag on and in many cases it's ignored."

"I think you'll probably get more traditional players now who give more **realistic pricing** expectations to their investors."

The overall response was probably typified by this comment: "At the end of the day, anything like this has to be driven at the demand end, from consumers. We're beginning to see this now in the market, from some of the multinationals, for example. But for it to be effective, it has to be led by the individual purchaser who says, 'I'm prepared to pay extra.' And that mind-set is a long way away."

Secular Trend Toward Higher Yields, Lower Prices?

In the short term, property prices in Asia (as elsewhere) are bound to fall simply as a factor of current macro and market forces. But in the aftermath, one question looms large: does the widening of yields we are now seeing represent a secular shift toward lower prices? A couple of factors point toward this conclusion. First, one of the main catalysts for the ultra-compressed yields seen in recent years was the phenomenon of the highly leveraged deal. In the newly deleveraged world, however, there will be less room for highly speculative players such as hedge funds, for whom property assets will become less attractive. The possible exception will be Japan, where the cost of funds is traditionally very low. According to one investor, "I think there's an expected softening in prices and a lot of that will result from lower demand from leveraged buyers. They won't be able to get the returns they were expecting previously, and the people with equity will be demanding a higher return." Another observed: "A lot of the funds that came out in the last year or so said, 'We'll give you 25 percent returns' because they could get 95 percent leverage on every deal. Those funds shouldn't have been in the real estate game to begin with. They're buying Microsoft shares one day and they'll be financing some real estate project the next—it doesn't make sense. I think you'll probably get more traditional players now who give more realistic pricing expectations to their investors."

Second, banks (and probably investors too) have already rerated property sector risk. According to one fund manager, "Probably the greatest impact of the problems on Wall Street is that the cap rates in Asia, which were probably some of the lowest in the world, are now starting to widen." In the past, "Asia didn't really price in risk, so construction financing versus completed, fully tenanted, grade A asset building financing were almost the same. I think banks took the view that these are big corporate clients and they'll eventually pay back anyway, so it was more relationship lending versus fundamental real estate lending." That now has changed. "In the future, Asian banks are likely to price deals according to a global standard. Bank financing is now stricter in terms of both the leverage and the rates charged, while covenants in the bank documents are now much more rigorous. Absolutely, this will be a long-term thing. It's a new reality."

海证券大厦
SHANGHAI STOCK EXCHANGE BUILDING
推PUSH

Real Estate Capital Flows

Current conditions favor those with **deep pockets,** clean balance sheets, and good connections with potential lenders.

The huge dislocations experienced in global financial markets over the course of 2008 have had a convulsive impact on institutions around the region whose job it is to pump capital into property investments. Be it bank lending, stock market equity, or debt capital, regional money flows constricted gradually over the course of the year until, as the markets crashed in early October, the cash stopped flowing altogether. Quickly jump-started by the central bank liquidity paddles, markets have revived enough for investors to find a pulse, but there can be no doubt regarding the diagnosis: this was the financial equivalent of coronary thrombosis.

While Asia's markets will surely survive their near-death experience, the prognosis for Asian capital flows in 2009 remains grim. The real estate sector can expect little relief from the current weakness in conventional mechanisms for delivering capital to investors, and while there is no doubt that opportunities from distressed sales will arise throughout the continent, finding ways to finance these purchases will remain challenging. Current conditions favor those with deep pockets, clean balance sheets, and good connections with potential lenders.

In the aftermath, there is equally little doubt that financial lifestyles will have to change before markets return eventually to good health. Commercial mortgage–backed securities (CMBS) and other derivative trades, already thin on the ground in Asia (apart from Japan), will probably not receive much of a second chance and will be subject to tighter regulation anyway. REITs, meanwhile, once the darling of real estate investors as an exit strategy for completed development projects, have fallen out of favor. Hard questions will be asked about how both equity and debt markets will value future investments in real estate. Finally, in perhaps the most profound lifestyle change of all, banks and borrowers will have to kick their addiction to leverage, a habit that got out of hand for too many investors seeking an easy option for outsized returns.

Banks Turn Off the Tap

Asia's banking system is especially important to real estate investors because the region's markets for alternative financing channels remain relatively immature. Compared with those in the West, Asia's debt and equity capital markets are both relatively small, while the market for derivatives, and especially for securitized debt, is smaller still. According to Morgan Stanley, lending from bank (32 percent) and nonbank (26 percent) institutions accounted for 57 percent of net private sector flows into global emerging markets between 2005 and 2008, with foreign direct investment (FDI) contributing 35 percent, and portfolio flows just 8 percent, of the total. On one level, this appears to be a dysfunctional means of allocating capital. At the same time, the very lack of sophistication in Asia's capital markets (with so little debt being securitized) is the most proximate reason why local banks have so far felt little of the pain inflicted on their peers in the West.

There are other factors too, though. For one, mortgage lending is still relatively new to many Asian markets and is therefore much smaller in proportion to the size of local economies than it is in Western countries. As a percentage

EXHIBIT 2-1

Change in Availability of Equity Capital for Real Estate by Source Type

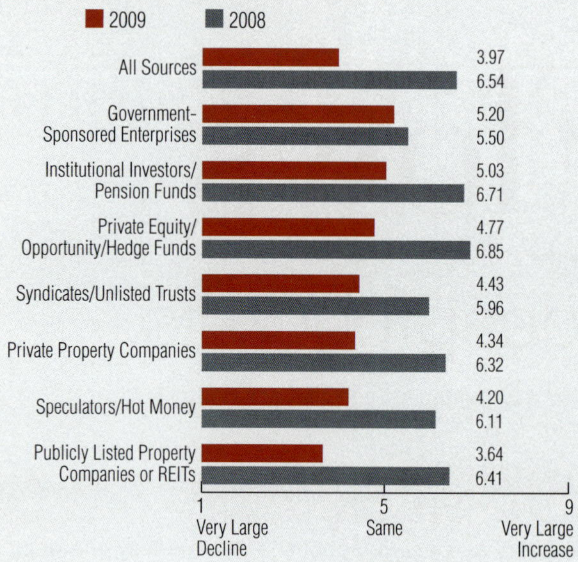

Source: *Emerging Trends in Real Estate Asia Pacific 2009* survey.

EXHIBIT 2-2

Equity Real Estate Capital Market Balance Prospects for 2009

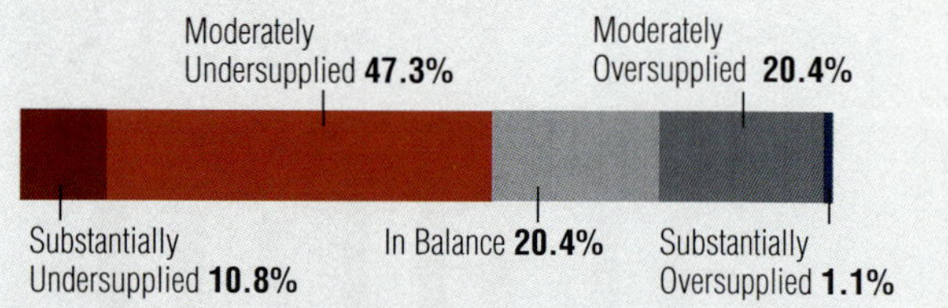

Source: *Emerging Trends in Real Estate Asia Pacific 2009* survey.

of gross domestic product (GDP), outstanding mortgages are equivalent to just 19 percent of Japan's economy, 12 percent of China's, and 5 percent of India's, according to investment bank CLSA. This is far different than in the United States, which has cumulative mortgage values that are almost 105 percent of their annual GDP. Second, Asian banks not only offer less property-related credit, but they also are more discriminating when handing it out. This is largely a byproduct of their experiences during the Asian financial crisis in 1997 when large numbers of banks imploded due to poor credit risk management and lending policy decisions. The scars from that time period include a legacy of risk aversion that survives a decade later (and may be a pointer to the future financial landscape in the West). Consumer-level mortgages, for example, are generally capped at 70 percent of property values, compared to rates of 80 to 100 percent common in the United States. In addition, banks have strong capital bases that shelter them from the vagaries of the market. As one interviewee says, "They have local currency in their own domicile, so it's not like they have to borrow in the swap market."

Perhaps the most important factor in all this, though, is cultural. There may be a bent toward speculation in Asia, but there is also a deep-rooted aversion to debt—at the consumer level, anyway (commercial lending may be another matter). The "charge it" mentality now so prevalent in developed countries never really took hold in Asia—and this makes a real difference. As the world deleverages, there should be less pain in places where there is less deleveraging to be done. That's the good news for Asia's banks and borrowers alike.

The bad news, though, is that with or without large quantities of indigenous toxic debt, the Asian banking sector is still hostage to events elsewhere. Borrowing used to be cheap in most of Asia, but as perceived risk began to inch up during the summer of 2007, borrowing costs rose along with it. Local institutions started to hike spreads at the end of 2007 and loans have since become progressively more expensive. According to one fund manager, "We always felt that the local banks in particular in most of the [Asian] markets priced real estate risk too low. What resulted from the subprime crisis is that banks looked at what real estate risk really was and thought maybe these construction loans at 80 basis points over SIBOR don't make any sense, and they really should be 250 or 275."

By the middle of 2008, a crisis of confidence had set in. Local banks may consider themselves well capitalized, but as the value of their collateral declines, their exposure increases. During the third quarter, they began to slam their doors shut as they scrambled to reduce levels of outstanding loans. By the time the crisis reached a crescendo at the end of September, banks were reluctant to lend even to each other, let alone their customers. For a week or so, the flow of credit froze up completely. Local interbank rates soared and even overnight rates became prohibitive, leaving most corporate borrowers to look elsewhere for funds. Liquidity injections from central banks soon thawed out frozen money markets, but going into the final quarter, regional banks are still reluctant to provide credit to anyone, especially those engaged in what are deemed to be riskier businesses such as small and medium-sized enterprises (SMEs) in general, or companies in the property sector.

And this is where the real risk lies—banks simply don't want to lend. There are problems, for example, in getting banks to issue even standard instruments of trade such as letters of credit, with the result that some exporters are refusing to ship goods because they have no guarantee of payment. In continuing to withhold credit from the market, banks risk generating another wave of macroeconomic pain as the crisis morphs from one of liquidity to one of solvency. Fears of counterparty credit risk may end up as a self-fulfilling prophecy if bank frugality—in Asia or elsewhere—pushes economies into a potentially deep recession, creating more bankruptcies and generating more defaults on large volumes of leveraged bank lending, even as it erodes the value of whatever collateral they hold.

Corporate earnings are already clearly deteriorating, and Asian banks have considerable exposure to many marginally profitable SMEs tied to the export sector that are today at greater risk of default. This is a much deeper pit than the one we were already in because it is more than just a question of confidence. Governments cannot deal with the problem by throwing money at it, as they don't have and can't borrow enough cash to fill the hole. Going forward, this will remain the biggest single issue affecting the real estate sector, both on a macro and a micro basis. As one investor said, "The real drive is going to come from the banks." Once they start lending money, things are going to be a lot easier for us—that's what we have to focus on." Unfortunately, that doesn't look likely anytime soon. By October, a few Asian banks were showing signs of stress. Large amounts of leveraged commercial lending have pushed out loan-to-deposit ratios in some countries, and especially at institutions in South Korea, India, and Thailand. The Korean market appears to be hurting the most, due to its large stock of maturing foreign currency borrowing and rapidly declining currency.

Meanwhile, credit risk management remains weak in countries like China, India, and Vietnam, where banks have little experience in real estate lending. Apparently, low bad-debt ratios may mask the fact that shallow property lending portfolios are expanding so rapidly in these places that new debts have not yet had a chance to go bad. According to one India-based consultant, "Indian bankers don't know how to deal with real estate credit. They will realize in about two years they made a lot of mistakes in assessing credit to Indian developers—the horror stories in the Indian real estate market, at least on the banking side, have still not come out." Should prices take a steeper turn, nonperforming loans (NPLs) in these countries may become significant, although for the reasons given above, this is unlikely in itself to pose a systemic risk.

Sentiment Is the Wild Card

Many fundamental factors influence the volume of capital flows, but sentiment sometimes trumps them all. Investor mood is always a big wildcard in Asia, and often creates volatile trading conditions. Hong Kong may prove to be a prime example of the impact of sentiment on a market with strong fundamentals. On paper, there seems little to suggest that property prices could freefall. A majority of homeowners have no debt, and the average mortgage span in the territory has fallen to around six years, meaning most potential purchasers are upgraders with little debt. Supply remains very tight on both the residential and office sides, the former because developers and government have colluded to prop up the market by withholding new supply, the latter because Hong Kong's traditional central business district (CBD) has basically run out of space. Interest rates remain low in both real and nominal terms. And yet, in a market historically prone to wild swings, it is hard to imagine real estate emerging unscathed after the local stock market dropped 70 percent in the year following its peak in October 2007. The fragility of investor confidence was illustrated by a run that took place on Hong Kong's third biggest (and apparently quite healthy) bank in September 2008, following a spate of SMS-spread rumors. In October, prices in both sectors were looking ominously fragile.

Governments Turn Off the Tap, Too

The drought in Asian bank lending is not driven just by the supply side. In several markets, credit contraction is a direct result of government policies seeking to restrain investment in overheated markets.

- In late 2007, Japanese authorities became leery of a potential bubble, particularly in residential real estate. They "basically told the banks to not lend—and they haven't." When the big international and investment banks suddenly closed up shop as the credit crunch began to bite at the beginning of 2008, they "left a pretty big void in the market because Japanese banks weren't willing to step up and fill the gap. That's ironic, because their balance sheets are as strong as they've been in years, if not decades."
- In China, meanwhile, rampant speculation and rapid price increases in property assets also led authorities to direct banks to cut property lending sharply to both developers and consumers in late 2007. The results were dramatic. In the first half of 2008, bank lending to developers and homebuyers declined 30 percent year on year. While official figures show Chinese property prices continuing to rise (albeit at a slower pace), anecdotal evidence suggests that prices have actually been in decline since early 2008, especially in the bigger cities. However, as the Chinese economy slows, the government has begun to ease the stranglehold over bank lending.
- In India, too, property sector lending was tightened in 2007 after the central bank became concerned about local banks' exposure to real estate loans. That leaves only private equity to fill the gap, and it isn't coming cheap. Cash-

strapped developers are now borrowing at sometimes astronomical rates—"behind the scenes, some developers are borrowing money at anything around 3 percent per month." Otherwise, "It's all mezzanine financing—high-cost stuff, where the fixed-return, preferred priority return component is as much as between 16 percent and 25 percent."

This spate of government-led capital squeezes explains not only why property prices have stalled in some Asian markets earlier than in others, but also why so many regional developers have been feeling the heat. In Japan, of the 17 listed companies seeking bankruptcy protection in 2008, 12 were either developers or directly related to the real estate sector. In both China and India, the cash crunch has hit early and hard, with hundreds of capital-constrained developers failing or now desperate for funding.

Capital Markets

While Asia's banks have so far gotten off relatively lightly from the credit convulsions, two other parts of the regional financial machine have not fared as well. Equity markets across Asia have been hard hit, sinking in tandem with U.S. markets since late 2007. The MSCI AC Asia Pacific Index, a composite of major Asian markets, dropped 50 percent in one year from its peak in October 2007. Shares of developers have been among the worst affected. The Hang Seng Property Index, which tracks Hong Kong's biggest developers, lost 60 percent of its value in the year ending November 2008. The slide is partly due to a huge selloff by foreign investors dumping their shareholdings of Asian stocks. Unsurprisingly, very few real estate–related companies have managed to list shares in this environment, with just US$5 billion worth of deals in Asia in the first half of 2008, compared to US$25 billion for the same period in 2007. In Japan, the number of new listings for property-related companies sank from 27 in 2006, to 15 in 2007, and just three in the first half of 2008. That's not many, but it's three more than in China. While ten Chinese property developers went public in Hong Kong in 2007, raising a record US$8.3 billion, the easy-money window closed in 2008, with at least 20 developers on the outside looking in by the middle of the year, and a similarly crowded field lined up in India. The problems in raising capital are reflected in our survey responses, with 68 percent of respondents stating that equity capital markets will be undersupplied in 2009. Developers still occasionally try their luck by announcing their intention to launch initial public offerings (IPOs), but plans have usually fallen through and there seems little prospect of major land-related listings as long as current conditions persist.

EXHIBIT 2-3

Debt Real Estate Capital Market Balance Prospects for 2009

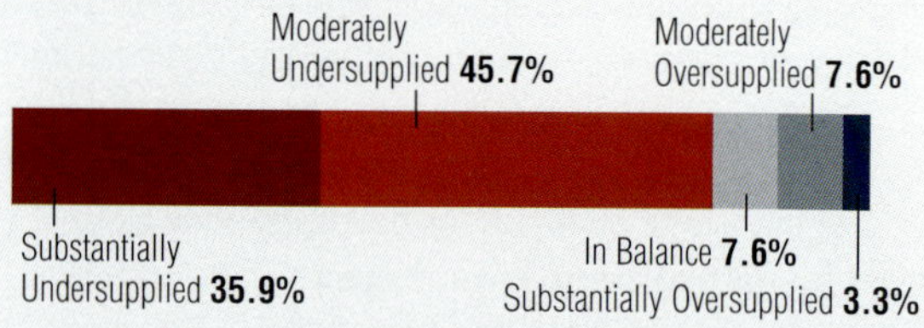

Source: *Emerging Trends in Real Estate Asia Pacific 2009* survey.

Offshore bond markets, meanwhile, have seen business fall off a cliff. As seen in Exhibit 2-3, the extremity of the debt drought comes through in the *Emerging Trends* survey, with some 82 percent of respondents predicting that capital debt markets will remain moderately or substantially undersupplied through 2009. Although Asia's reliance on the offshore funding market is not nearly as high as it is in other regions, risk premiums on dollar-denominated bonds from Asian issuers have risen sharply, with spreads widening markedly since mid-2007, as risk aversion in Asia catches up with the rest of the world. Issuance slowed to a crawl in the final quarter of 2007 and effectively ground to a halt about a year later. Credit for some types of borrowing, such as junk bonds, was shut off earlier. Ominously, however, even after the Fed bailout, spreads have continued to widen, indicating a lack of confidence in the market that the economic tide has not turned. Near the end of October, the iTraxx Asia (excluding Japan) HY index, a credit default swap (CDS) benchmark measuring the cost of insuring offshore high-yield bonds, traded at an amazing 1,300 basis points to 1,500 basis points, having risen fivefold over the year. The wide spread (which usually reflects perceived risk) may seem odd given the strong balance sheets and lack of defaults in traded names in Asia, but it reflects the impact of redemptions by international investors trying to unwind positions as they continue to deleverage, combined with reluctance to buy at any level amid fears of rising defaults among emerging market corporate borrowers. It may also reflect concerns over the impact of potential currency declines in Asian markets. Since July 2008, the previously weak U.S. dollar has appreciated considerably against emerging market currencies as investors bring funds back to the United States or simply convert to the dollar as a safe haven. This significantly increases the quantum of dollar-denominated debt repayments owed by local bond issuers.

The markets for local-currency bonds, while not as big as those for U.S. dollar–denominated issues, were at first beneficiaries of the crisis, as investors fled the United States in search of higher yields. But hopeful borrowers soon crowded into the space, and competition for funds became intense. More recently, these markets (especially the larger ones such as Japan and Korea) have also retrenched, although they continue to offer more liquidity than the offshore market and will probably continue to do so.

Today, bond spreads in Asian markets have gone out so far that debt buybacks should represent compelling value for many property companies. Assuming they have the financial strength to survive the downturn, debt repurchases offer developers implied yields better (at between 30 and 60 percent) than they would be likely to earn from developing property. So far, however, most Asian companies have been slow to repurchase debt, preferring instead to focus on share buybacks. Nonetheless, the debt markets still represent compelling opportunities for investors with strong stomachs and the right analytical skills. According to one Singapore-based fund manager, "Twelve months ago, the spreads on private debt were very thin and a lot of investors found it too expensive—now we have a situation where even some of the investment banks are selling the debt to get it off their balance sheet at significant discounts."

EXHIBIT 2-4

Markit iTraxx Asia HY Index (Excluding Japan)

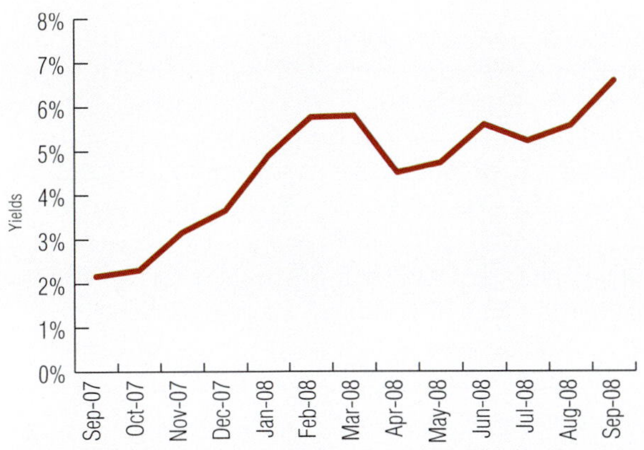

Source: Markit Group Limited.

Cash-Strapped Developers Hunt for Funds

With cash so tight, regional developers have been scratching around looking for capital. But in a sector where financing has traditionally been dominated by the banks, they have often come up short. With the IPO market long since closed, they turned first to the offshore debt market. Today, though, the offshore-debt door is welded shut. Expensive convertible bonds remain one of the few channels where significant offshore funding for developers may still available.

Although they mean paying internal rates of return as high as 15 to 20 percent, as many as 40 unlisted Chinese developers have taken on such structured investments in 2007 and 2008. A few are funding construction with equity.

The logjam in the capital markets has added momentum to an ongoing trend for "increasingly concerned and, potentially, increasingly desperate" developers to pair up directly with equity investors. Ironically, until now the driving force behind such marriages had come from the investor side. With so much private capital sloshing around Asia in 2006 and 2007, competition to get money into the market was intense, and funds would commonly turn up looking for a piece of the action. Now, though, the shoe is on the other foot. Investors can afford to be picky, and they need to be, as the landscape is treacherous and they are generally operating outside their comfort zones. As one consultant says, "Project delivery is a challenge. The human factor plays a huge part and a number of projects either have taken much longer or cost much more because they haven't been able either to manage the cost or manage the program." Nonetheless, in 2007, the value of merger and acquisition (M&A) deals involving Chinese property companies was US$21 billion. In the first half of 2008, deal volumes had risen to some US$15.3 billion, according to Dealogic, while developers had tapped into foreign capital sources for some US$6.1 billion, according to official figures, up 22 percent on the year.

In addition, bigger developers are also finding takeovers of smaller players an interesting option. In part, this is because takeovers offer a cheap way to add to their land banks, and in part because takeovers provide an opportunity to add to their pool of skilled labor, itself a scarce resource in Asia. As one consultant observed, "Every developer of any size is stretched for people, so they're quite interested in acquiring other companies just to get their staff."

As the financing squeeze extends across Asia over the next year or so, the pool of developers will inevitably shrink. Some may be absorbed by bigger players; many more will go bust. Given the very high number of small developers out there, especially in developing countries (China alone had some 50,000 of them at the end of 2007), the bloodletting may be intense. As one investor in Japan commented: "Many of these small to medium-sized developers that are so far over their skis were borrowing hand over fist hoping for a white knight to buy their wholly mediocre, wholly misconceived product. That's not going to happen, those days are gone. And you can't help but wonder whether that's a good thing."

Global Funds Coming and Going

In recent years, Asian property markets have received ever-larger flows of capital originating from both elsewhere in Asia and throughout the world. Japan has been the most important recipient, ending up with about half of the total in 2007. Otherwise, intra-Asian investors (principally from Hong Kong and Singapore) are big buyers of development sites in China, while global buyers tend to focus on completed office projects, again in China. In 2007, the total of all cross-border investment in Asian commercial real estate was US$121 billion, up 27 percent on the previous year, according to Jones Lang LaSalle. However, that number is certain to have shrunk in 2008, and there must be some doubt as to whether such strong capital flows can be sustained in a future environment featuring much higher levels of perceived risk and much lower levels of leverage. Indeed, the *Emerging Trends* survey suggests that lower amounts of equity will arrive from all source countries in 2009, with contributions from the Middle East the only ones to increase, and the United States showing the biggest drop. By investor type, government-sponsored enterprises are the biggest contributors, followed by pension and private equity funds. REITs bring up the rear by a fairly wide margin.

EXHIBIT 2-5

Change in Availability of Equity Capital for Real Estate by Source Location

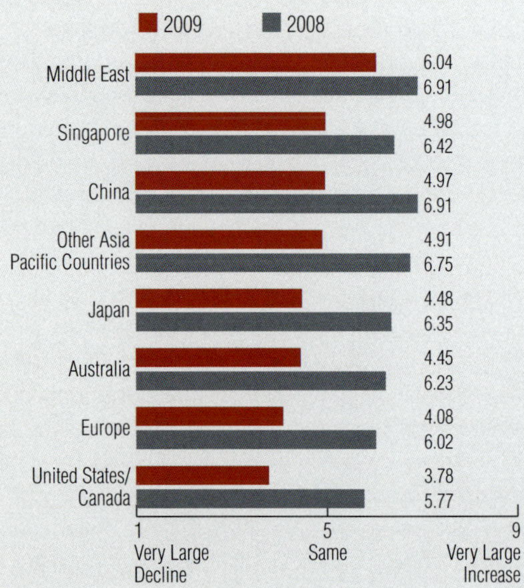

Source: *Emerging Trends in Real Estate Asia Pacific 2009* survey.

EXHIBIT 2-6

Investment Prospects by Asset Class for 2009

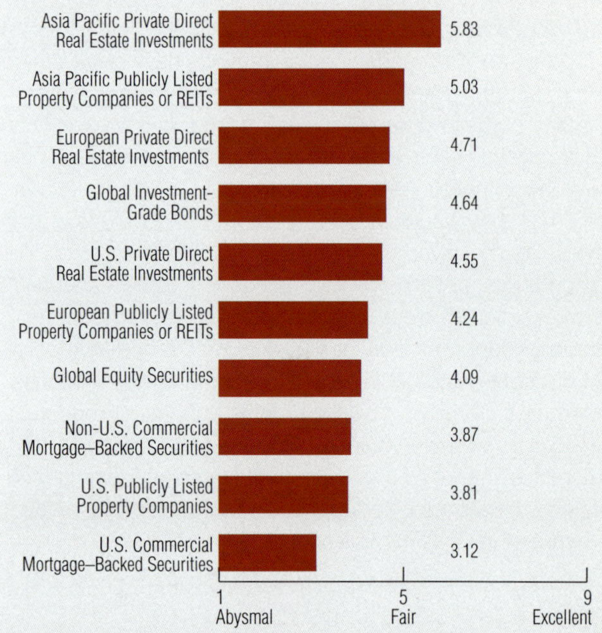

Source: *Emerging Trends in Real Estate Asia Pacific 2009* survey.

While cross-border capital certainly provides more liquidity to real estate markets, it also creates a risk of violent dislocations if funds are suddenly withdrawn in the aftermath of a crisis such as the current one. In this case, as global investors rush to deleverage and cut risk, they have sold vast quantities of offshore assets, many from Asia and many relating to real estate holdings. For example, all major Asian markets except for Japan, Vietnam, and Indonesia have recorded net foreign portfolio outflow from local equity markets in 2008, according to investment bank Standard Chartered. The total value of all outgoing capital flows is currently difficult to assess, but their magnitude can be guessed at via swings in currency values, with the dollar spiking as investors sell foreign currency assets.

Still, Asia continues to be seen as a good place for real estate investors to diversify away from beleaguered Western markets because it may be about the only place left with good short-term prospects: "It's the place with the fundamental growth, the extraordinary demographic changes, and these urbanization phenomena—these drive certain classes of real estate." New investors looking for

EXHIBIT 2-7

Largest Sovereign Funds by Assets

Country	Fund Name	Assets (US$ Billions)	Inception
U.A.E.—Abu Dhabi	Abu Dhabi Investment Authority	875	1976
Norway	Government Pension Fund	397	1990
Saudi Arabia	SAMA Foreign Holdings	365	N/A
Singapore	GIC	330	1981
China	SAFE Investment Company	312	N/A
Kuwait	Kuwait Investment Authority	264	1953
China	China Investment Corp.	200	2007
Hong Kong	Hong Kong Monetary Authority Investment Portfolio	173	1998
Russia	National Welfare Fund	163	2008
Singapore	Temasek Holdings	134	1974

Source: Sovereign Wealth Fund Institute.

growth opportunities are still turning up in Asia to kick the real estate tires. Anecdotally, the volume of real estate investment funds coming into Asia still outweighs flows moving the other way.

Petrodollars and Sovereign Funds

Identifying the sources of international capital these days is a thankless business, given the truly global nature of international finance. However, there are two especially noteworthy sources of external funding being deployed in Asia. The first is petrodollars from the Middle East and other oil-producing states. With oil dipping below US$70 per barrel, the value of exports from Gulf states will total US$6.2 trillion over the next 14 years, according to consultants McKinsey & Co., more than triple the amount earned over the last 14 years. After accounting for domestic investment, at least US$3.5 trillion of this is likely to be invested externally. While in the past, much of the money coming out of the Middle East was channeled into core assets in the United States and Europe, the bias is now shifting in favor of Asian assets. According to one fund manager with experience of Gulf state investment strategies, "The gravity of the last adjustment may have made a number of these investors think more holistically about the real estate universe and that includes Asia, which is probably the next region after the United States and Europe that many of the more sophisticated Middle East investors will choose to invest." Asia's share of petrodollar investment allocations is likely to increase from 10 to 20 percent by 2020, says McKinsey. That translates into a huge new stream of funding that is already finding its way into Asian real estate assets, especially in India, Malaysia, and China. According to one consultant, "They offer a very interesting alternative source of capital for developers. The bulk of them act as equity players. Deals we've been involved with have either been project specific or sitting alongside the developer and taking a share across all its portfolio, either through buying shares or providing a pool of equity that he uses, then given shares by way of return."

In theory, sovereign wealth funds also will benefit from the market dislocations. With huge amounts of capital on tap, they have little need to use large amounts of debt and are good credit risks if they want it. New entrants are now bringing bulging pockets to the table. These include at least two Chinese funds bearing a portion of Beijing's US$1.9 trillion in foreign currency reserves. Middle East funds also are cashed up in petrodollars. Historically, most sovereign wealth funds have focused their buying on developed market bond and equities markets. But low returns, resulting especially from the long decline in the value of the U.S. dollar, in which most of their investing has been concentrated, has led to growing interest in different asset classes. Property investment is an obvious candidate given that its long-term investment characteristics match well with sovereign fund requirements. Some sovereign wealth funds, such as the Government of Singapore Investment Corp. (GIC), are already large and active buyers of real estate, although historically investment has been concentrated in mature markets.

According to one investor, "Our info is that these funds that invest in real estate invest offshore. Their focus is picking up distressed assets in the U.S. and Europe and they're positioning themselves for that opportunity, although Asia is also on their radars. Again, though, none of them thinks [that]

EXHIBIT 2-8

Asia and Australia CMBS Issuance

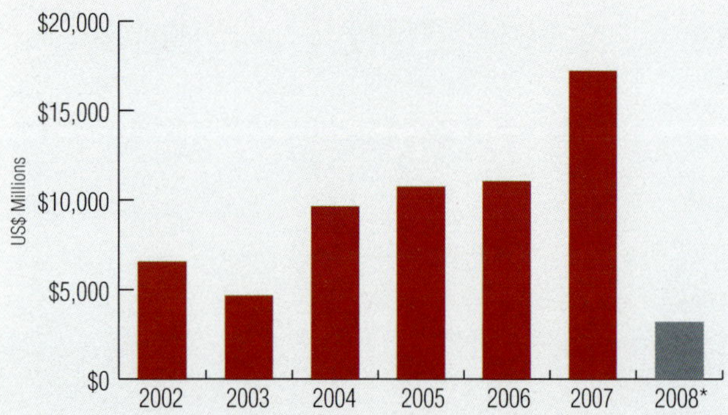

Source: Commercial Mortgage Alert.

* Total issuance as of September 30, 2008.

now is quite the right time—they probably will appear 12 months or so out from here." Another interviewee said: "I'm probably not as bullish on sovereign wealth funds coming in as some. They're not going to be in any rush. They know they have capital and not many people do. I don't imagine they're going to be there underpinning the rest of the market. They're looking for quality and I don't think that those holding quality assets are going to be that eager to sell."

Although a lack of transparency makes their investment strategies difficult to analyze, a recent report from consultants CBRE estimated that a 7 percent allocation into real estate assets by these funds would be a reasonable assumption, translating to around US$165 billion worth of property investment based on their current cash holdings of about US$4 trillion. Looking forward, a likely sovereign wealth fund asset base of some US$12 trillion by 2015 (as projected by investment bank Morgan Stanley) would mean a further US$560 billion of new capital sunk into property purchases.

More recently, however, the prospects of sovereign wealth funds becoming big buyers of emerging market real estate have waned. Not only have some funds been burnt by purchases of investment bank stocks at prices far higher than they are now, but many are now said to be looking to their domestic markets to prop up prices as currencies plunge against the dollar and cross-border bank financing dries up.

CMBS

While traded derivative debt is a generally new phenomenon in Asian markets, it has grown strongly since a surge in regional bond issuance in 2006. Credit-risk innovations such as single-name CDS contracts appeared, together with actively traded CDS indices, both sovereign and high yield. Asian investors have shown little interest in the MBS sector, however, apart from in Japan, where CMBS is the largest source of commercial property finance, with issuance approaching 40 percent of all sales, according to RCA. The value of new CMBS issuance in Asia amounted to some US$17.2 billion in 2007, of which US$14.8 billion originated in Japan.

There have been very few CMBS defaults in Japan, but spreads on AAA-rated CMBS widened considerably over the course of 2008. By October, some US$3 billion in CMBS deals had been completed for the year. As important as CMBS have become in Japan, however, the derivatives market was always a playground for the international banks. According to one interviewee, CMBS deals "were all being done by international banks and lots of the buyers were Japanese or European institutions. Last year, Japanese banks were not originating a whole lot of paper for securitization. Under current regulations in Japan, if you're a buyer you have to do due diligence on every item in the portfolio. These departments have a small staff and so don't have the ability to do it unless it's just one or two assets. So now people doing are large, single-office asset securitizations instead."

Will the CMBS market survive in Japan? Says one consultant, "I think it has to. What's the alternative? Going back to the old balance sheet/portfolio lending model? In this marketplace, which banks would be able to do so and not blow their capital adequacy requirements? I think it will be a lot more regulated, and that's probably a good thing, but it will need to reemerge."

REITs

The two biggest REIT markets in Asia remain Japan and Australia, although stock markets in both Singapore and Hong Kong also have a significant number of traded REITs. Most recently, India has just introduced real estate mutual funds, which are essentially REITs in disguise. These are expected to provide a more diverse range of investment vehicles and a good channel for foreign capital to get exposure to Indian real estate through the equity markets.

EXHIBIT 2-9

Asia Pacific CMBS by Collateral Location

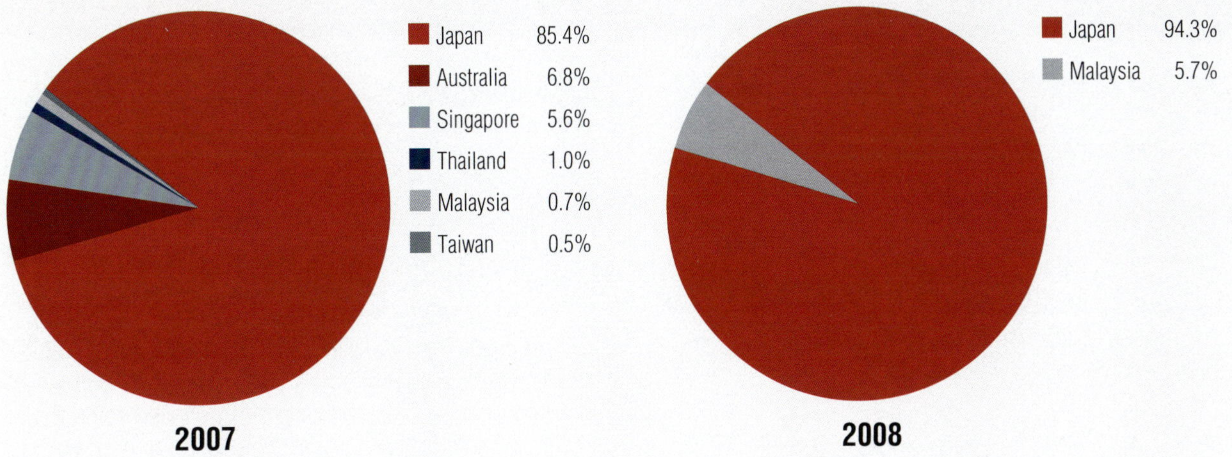

Source: Commercial Mortgage Alert. Transaction volume in U.S. dollars.

* Total issuance as of September 30, 2008.

EXHIBIT 2-10

Asia Pacific CMBS Issuance by Property Type

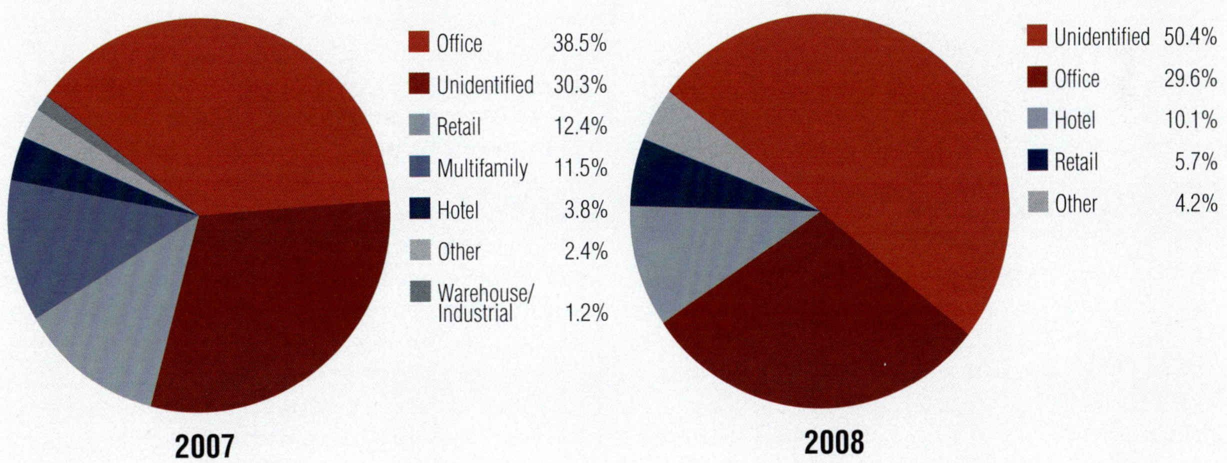

Source: Commercial Mortgage Alert. Transaction volume in U.S. dollars.

* Total issuance as of September 30, 2008.

EXHIBIT 2-11

Listed Property and REIT Market Capitalization

	S&P/Citigroup	
	Global Property Index (US$ Millions)	Global REIT Index (US$ Millions)
Global	922,488	514,501
North America	313,666	296,031
Asia Pacific	342,754	113,366
Europe	150,652	100,679
Hong Kong	124,077	8,110
Japan	115,274	31,104
Australia	66,037	60,221
China	53,366	0
Singapore	35,400	11,965
India	18,431	0
Philippines	6,119	0
Taiwan	4,560	1,189
Thailand	4,222	0
Malaysia	3,571	286
New Zealand	1,966	1,966
Indonesia	1,613	0

Source: S&P/Citigroup Global Equity Indicies. All data as of September 30, 2008.

While REITs used to be considered the golden child of Asian real estate, much of the shine has come off in 2008, with dramatic declines in REIT stock prices throughout the region. By the end of October, Japan's J-REIT index, for example, had fallen 70 percent since its peak in May 2007. In Australia, highly leveraged listed property trusts (LPTs) have faced steep hikes in borrowing costs as debt spreads widened in 2008. The problem has been exacerbated by the collapse of the Australia dollar, forcing funds with dollar-denominated debt to sell assets in order to make interest payments. Otherwise, REITs face problems from a couple of angles. In the past, according to one REIT manager in Singapore, yield compression made it hard for REITs to buy assets "because the environment is such that our distribution yield as a REIT is higher than what the property will yield." Unable to make accretive assets, REITs were basically dead in the water as they sought to expand. Today, although yields have started to widen, REIT stock prices have been crushed, at least partly because "the hedge funds that held a lot of the REITs have started to dump their shares significantly." Falling share prices inflate distribution yields, so that any new purchases tend still to be dilutive, even though cap rates trends have reversed. On top of that comes the credit crunch, which means REITs "have to think very laterally in how you are financing these deals. You have to look at all the products and pull out all your relationships to make it work—you can't just go to a bank and borrow on a mortgage. So the REITs are coming up with interesting strategies to solve the problem—convertible bonds, Shariah-compliant bonds. It's all debt because we can't go out to the equity market to raise money."

While these trends have put Asian REITs in a bind, their exceptionally low share prices now represent good fundamental value, with many now boasting double-digit yields. According to one fund manager, "I definitely think the REITs are a good investment because they are trading so low. Theoretically, if you can buy a liquid stock where it's trading at a discount and in some cases 50 to 60 percent to NAV, you're far better to be buying the stocks than the real estate itself." Says another investor: "Property tends to be an emotional asset class, and I think a lot of them are trapped in the whirlwind. When the dust settles, I think you'll find a spike in value."

REITs' low NAVs have spawned much talk of privatizations or takeovers, particularly of the management companies. According to one Hong Kong–based consultant, "I think we'll see REITs taken private, and it will be a story around the region. Property development doesn't really lend itself to a six- or 12-month cycle valuation, it's a three- or four-year program and in a way you want to be able to maneuver or mix and match within that period." Of course, privatizing REITs would eliminate a traditional avenue for exiting investments that was once touted as one of the main reasons for the creation of a REIT industry. "Previously, you had to build and hold or you strata-titled because there wasn't an exit. But now we have a whole range of ways to exit, from securitization to private funds to public funds." REITs used to be an attractive exit strategy for developers: "The way they were priced and financially structured was attractive for a couple of years, but thereafter if you parted the curtains it became clear the upside was a bit limited." As a result, "there's not much in the pipeline for listed REITs, but what you're getting is the equivalent of a lot of private REITs being created. You package them in the same way as a public REIT, then you offer them to a consortium and they become the retailers. You have private shareholders rather

"Property tends to be an emotional asset class, and I think a lot of them are trapped in the **whirlwind.** When the dust settles, I think you'll find a **spike** in value."

than public shareholders. Then, you can pick and choose shareholders and there's more likely to be a situation where there's a commonality of purpose and interest."

In fact, talk of privatization is rife throughout the property industry generally. "When your NAV is half that of the real world, it means that one of the stories over the next two to three years is privatization, and not just of REITs. I sat in on several meetings with major Chinese developers who are looking very seriously at privitizations because they've only IPO'd three or four years, and most of their shares are held by three or four major institutions that underpinned them when they did the launch, so privatization would not be all that difficult. If you offer the major investor a 20 percent markup on its current share value, he's still looking pretty compared to the IPO situation."

僕の歩く道

Markets and Sectors to Watch

For 2009, it's time to be "picky about markets and partners."

According to this year's interviewees, real estate's well-known mantra of "location, location, location" has a new twist—"focus, focus, focus." For 2009, it's time to be "picky about markets and partners," as one survey respondent simply stated. Focus on core cities and on existing investments and developments, and enlarge and expand cautiously are two of the major trends emerging from this year's survey. In addition to increased focus on the part of survey respondents and interviewees, top trends for markets and property sectors include the following:

- Tokyo, Singapore, and Shanghai consistently ranked in the top ten markets for investment three years in a row.
- Sydney, Auckland, Osaka, and Melbourne rank in the top ten city risk ratings, but not in the top ten for investment or development.
- The office sector ranks first for investment and development prospects for 2009.
- Buy recommendations are consistently down across all property sectors, especially for hotel and office, with dramatic decreases for all markets.

One can clearly see the effects of global economic and financial challenges and issues at the city level. In the current environment, Asia Pacific cities are no less susceptible than cities in Europe, Latin America, the Middle East, and North America. As insecurity and concerns abound for investors, developers, and lenders, it is perhaps wise not to stray too far from one's areas of expertise and geography in 2009. Will this have an effect on cross-border investment levels in 2009? Will Asia Pacific cities that recovered first after the 1997 Asian financial crisis be the first to show signs of life in 2009?

Wishful Thinking

Survey respondents still envision more maturity, less cyclical markets, and improved transparency across all Asia Pacific cities in the near future. According to one interviewee, part of improved focus for 2009 is the relationship between infrastructure and real estate: "In the Asia Pacific region, only Japan, Australia, and Singapore have already established enough infrastructure for real estate investment and development. But in the next five years, other countries will catch up with the preceding three." Perhaps this pan–Asia Pacific investor is indirectly encouraging domestic capital sources in emerging markets to develop infrastructure in the near term.

Similar to the ups and downs of global stock markets, this year's survey respondents and interviewees recognize significant differences between emerging cities such as Ho Chi Minh City and mature cities such as Tokyo. Survey respondents rank Tokyo, Singapore, and Hong Kong first, second, and third in investment prospects respectively in 2009 as listed in Exhibit 3-1. The remaining cities in the top ten investment prospect rankings, with the exception of Shanghai and Seoul, are new entrants to the top ten rankings. New entrants include Bangalore, Mumbai, Taipei, New Delhi, and Kuala Lumpur.

EXHIBIT 3-1
City Investment Prospects

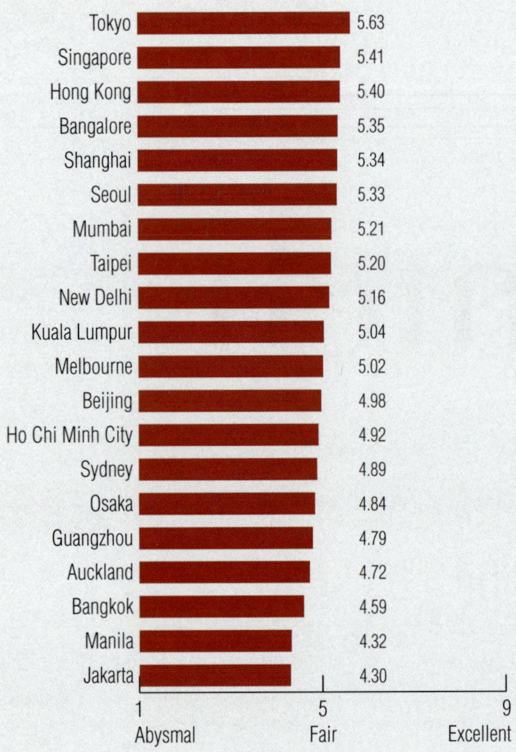

Source: *Emerging Trends in Real Estate Asia Pacific 2009* survey.

EXHIBIT 3-2
2009 vs. 2008 Investment Prospect

City	2009	2008	2007
Tokyo	1	3	3
Singapore	2	2	4
Hong Kong	3	5	11
Bangalore	4	12	10
Shanghai	5	1	2
Seoul	6	7	13
Mumbai	7	10	17
Taipei	8	16	5
New Delhi	9	13	14
Kuala Lumpur	10	11	15
Melbourne	11	17	6
Beijing	12	6	9
Ho Chi Minh City	13	8	12
Sydney	14	15	16
Osaka	15	4	1
Guangzhou	16	9	7
Auckland	17	14	NA
Bangkok	18	18	8
Manila	19	19	18
Jakarta	20	20	19

Sources: *Emerging Trends in Real Estate Asia Pacific 2009* and *2008* surveys.

EXHIBIT 3-3
City Risk Ratings

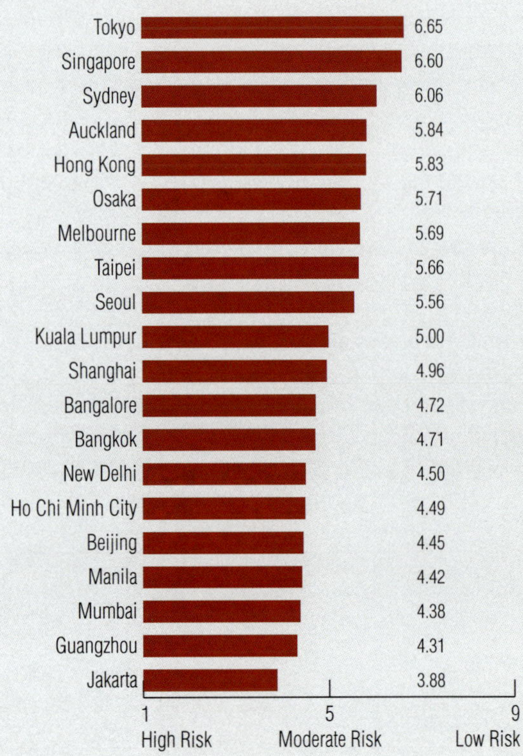

Source: *Emerging Trends in Real Estate Asia Pacific 2009* survey.

Consistency Is the Key Measure

Exhibit 3-2 illustrates investment rankings from 2007 to 2009. There is significant correlation between 2009 and 2008 rankings, but insignificant correlation between 2009 and 2007 rankings. Only three cities are in the top ten investment rankings for the last three years: Tokyo, Singapore, and Shanghai. Hong Kong, Seoul, Mumbai, New Delhi, and Kuala Lumpur have consistently moved up in the rankings over the past three years.

Exhibit 3-3 lists city risk ratings; higher ratings indicate low risks and low ratings indicate high risks. Survey respondents rate several of the top ten investment prospect cities such as Tokyo, Singapore, Hong Kong, Taipei, Seoul, and Kuala Lumpur also in the top ten city risk ratings. There are, however, cities such as Sydney, Auckland, Osaka, and Melbourne that rank in the top ten city risk ratings, but not in the top ten investment prospect ratings.

EXHIBIT 3-4

City Development Prospects

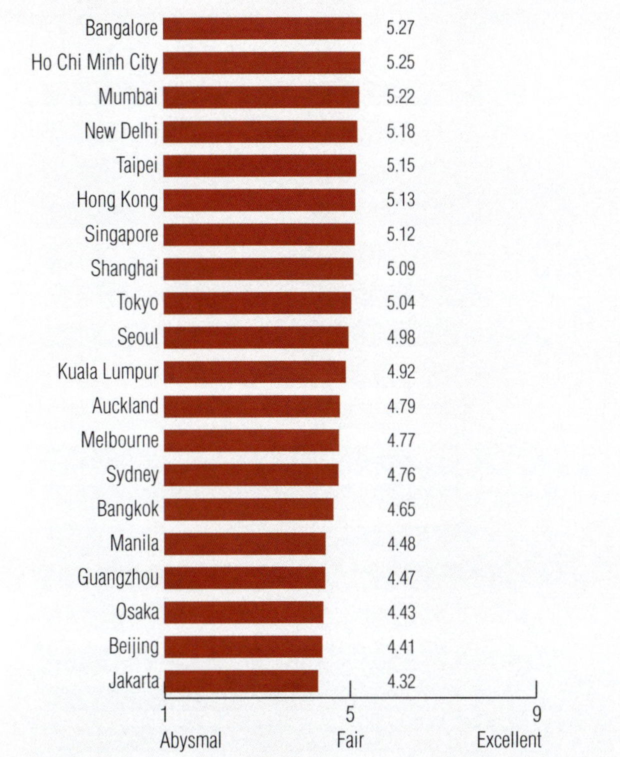

Source: *Emerging Trends in Real Estate Asia Pacific 2009* survey.

Combining the survey respondents' city risk ratings in Exhibit 3-3 with results in Exhibits 3-1 and 3-4 offers additional analysis that provides insight into Asia Pacific markets in 2009. For example, investment, development, and city risk rankings vary widely for markets such as Bangalore (fourth, first, 12th), Mumbai (seventh, third, 18th), New Delhi (ninth, fourth, 14th), and Ho Chi Minh City (13th, second, 15th), while other market such as Taipei (eighth, fifth, eighth) and Kuala Lumpur (tenth, 11th, tenth) are more consistent.

Property Types in Perspective

Survey respondents indicate that the office sector offers the highest rating for investment and development prospects for 2009. Exhibit 3-5 shows that the variance between the top and bottom property sectors in the investment prospect column is 90 basis points, whereas the range from top to bottom in the development prospect column is 39 basis points. Each property sector, with the exception of residential (for sale), has a higher investment rating than development, potentially reflecting the difficulty in securing development capital in 2009.

Expect cap rates to increase in 2009; "yields are gapping out in every market 50 to 100 basis points," although survey respondents indicate slightly lower spreads from August 2008 to December 2009 (see Exhibit 3-6).

Key investment properties, like office and retail, will show investment and development growth in first-tier cities; however, the residential market will focus more on second- and third-tier cities.

EXHIBIT 3-5

Real Estate Sector Performance Prospects for 2009

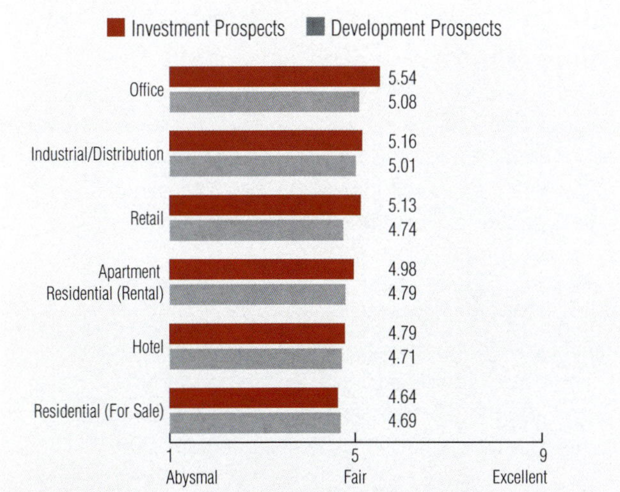

Source: *Emerging Trends in Real Estate Asia Pacific 2009* survey.

EXHIBIT 3-6

Real Estate Sector Prospects for Capitalization Rates

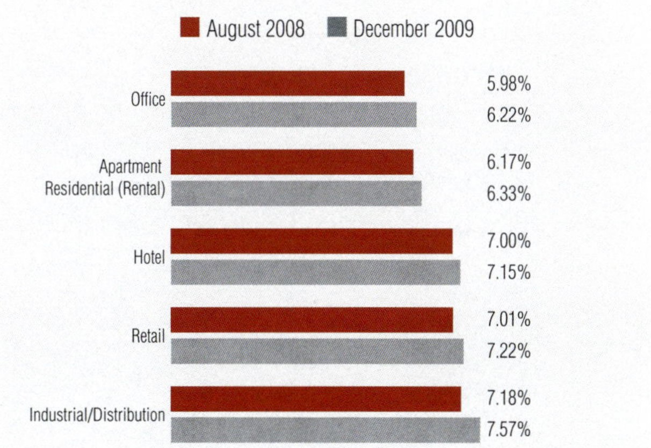

Source: *Emerging Trends in Real Estate Asia Pacific 2009* survey.

EXHIBIT 3-7
Hotel Property Buy/Hold/Sell Recommendations by City

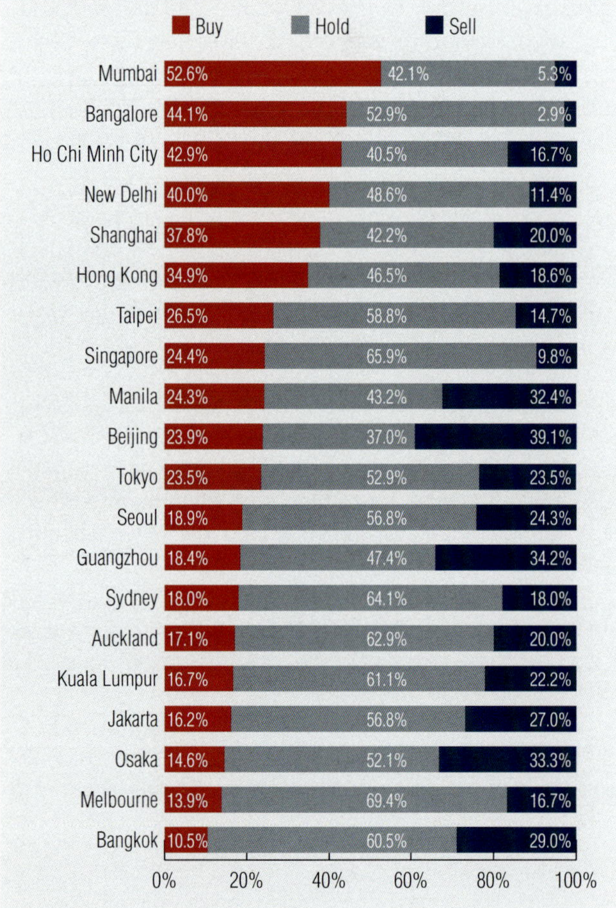

Source: *Emerging Trends in Real Estate Asia Pacific 2009* survey.

EXHIBIT 3-8
Office Property Buy/Hold/Sell Recommendations by City

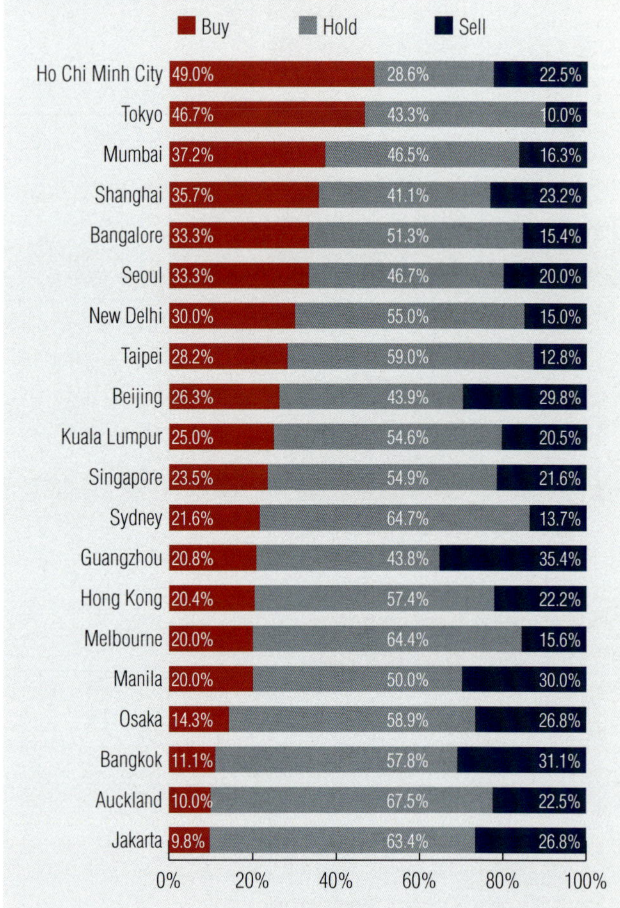

Source: *Emerging Trends in Real Estate Asia Pacific 2009* survey.

Hotel Sector: Reduced Buy Recommendations

Last year, survey respondents identified five hotel markets with over 60 percent buy recommendations. How quickly the world of hotel markets can change as this year's survey respondents do not identify even one market with such a high buy recommendation. For example, Ho Chi Minh City's buy recommendation has declined from 78.5 percent in 2008 to 42.9 percent for 2009, and Shanghai's buy recommendation has decreased from 64.6 percent in 2008 to 37.8 percent.

Office Sector

As with the hotel sector, the reduction in buy recommendations continues for the office sector. This year's survey respondents did not choose one office market higher than 50 percent for buy recommendations, whereas last year there were ten office markets with 50 percent or greater buy recommendations.

Sell recommendations for the two highest office vacancy rate markets (Exhibit 3-9), Beijing and Guangzhou, have significantly increased over 2008 levels. For example, Beijing's sell recommendation has jumped from 18.5 percent in 2008 to 29.8 percent in 2009; and Guangzhou's from 9.5 percent in 2008 to 35.4 percent in 2009.

EXHIBIT 3-9
Asia Pacific Office Vacancies

	Forecast (%) 2008*
Beijing	18.0
Shanghai (Pudong)	6.3
New Delhi	2.8
Bangalore	2.2
Mumbai	2.9
Kuala Lumpur	6.9
Bangkok	7.5
Taipei	6.6
Hong Kong	2.3
Seoul	0.2
Tokyo	2.0
Osaka	NA
Singapore	0.6
Sydney	2.8
Melbourne	3.3

Source: CB Richard Ellis.
* Data as of June 30, 2008.

EXHIBIT 3-10
Retail Property Buy/Hold/Sell Recommendations by City

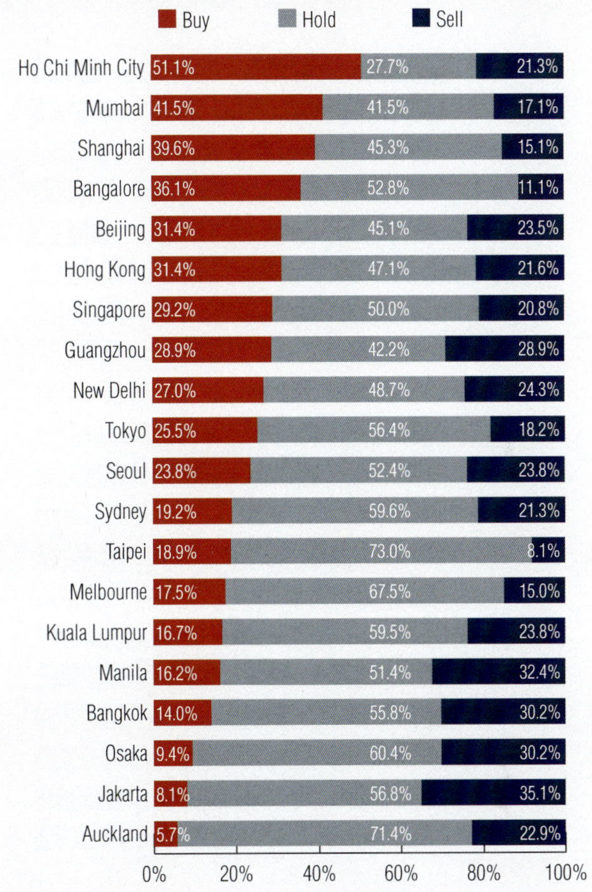

Source: *Emerging Trends in Real Estate Asia Pacific 2009* survey.

Retail Sector: Cautious Strategies

Survey respondents clearly point out the wide variations of buy, hold, and sell recommendations across Asia Pacific cities for 2009 for the retail sector. Buy recommendations range from a low of 5.7 percent in Auckland to a high of 51.1 percent in Ho Chi Minh City. Hold recommendations range from Taipei's 73.0 percent to Ho Chi Minh City's 27.7 percent, and sell recommendations range from a low of 8.1 percent in Taipei to 35.1 percent in Jakarta. Is it possible that, with such wide buy, hold, and sell variations, survey respondents are indirectly cautioning retail investors and developers as they formulate retail investment decisions and strategies for 2009?

Industrial Sector: Subdued Recommendations

The buy, hold, and sell recommendations for the industrial sector follow the pattern of previous property sectors. Compared with 2008's results, there is a consensus that 2009 is a year to hold industrial, reduce buy decisions, and sell in select markets. Seoul's sell recommendations have increased from 8.5 percent in 2008 to 33.3 percent in 2009, and even markets with high sell recommendations in 2008, such as Manila (18.5 percent in 2008), have experienced higher sell recommendations in 2009.

EXHIBIT 3-11

Industrial/Distribution Property Buy/Hold/Sell Recommendations by City

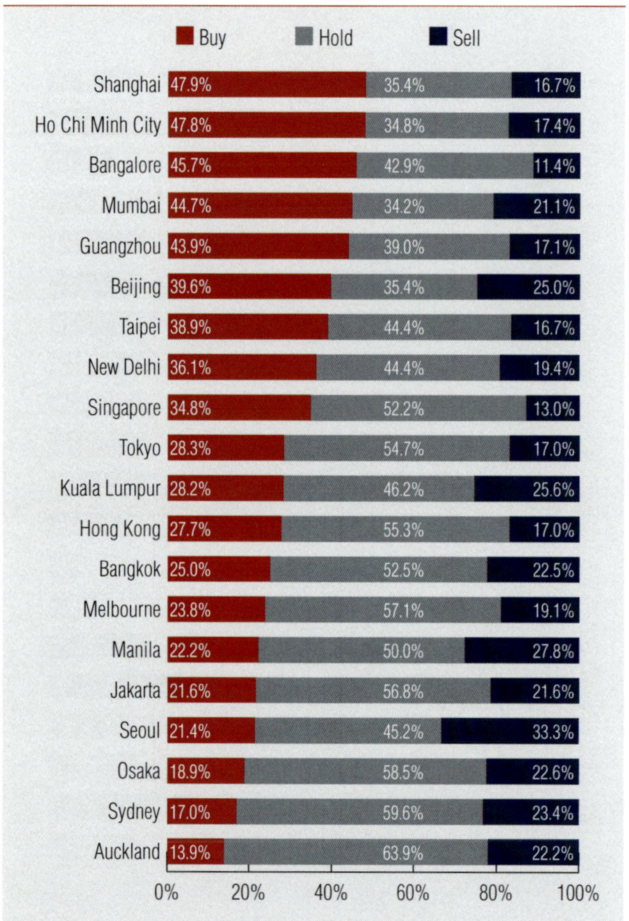

Source: *Emerging Trends in Real Estate Asia Pacific 2009* survey.

EXHIBIT 3-12

Apartment Residential (Rental) Property Buy/Hold/Sell Recommendations by City

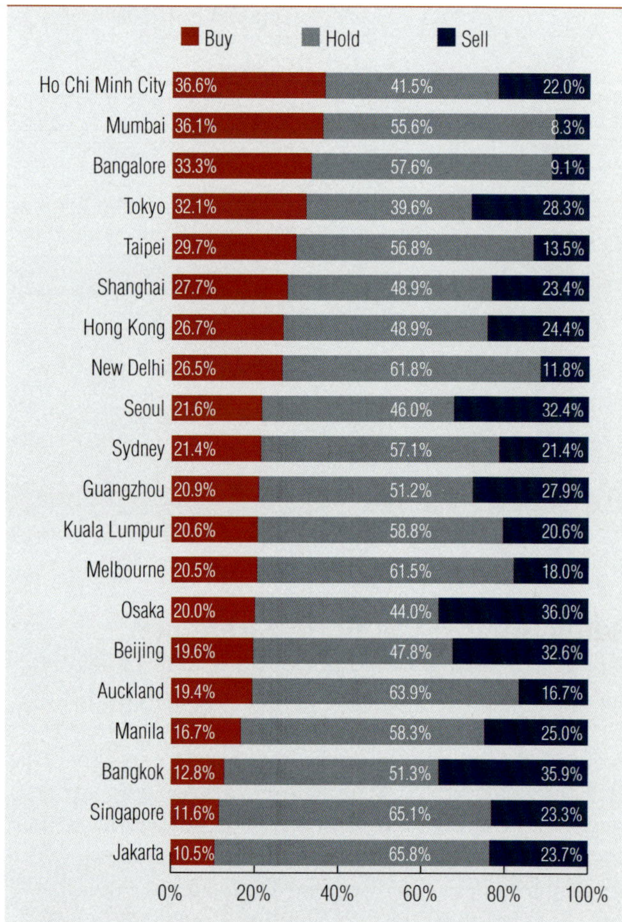

Source: *Emerging Trends in Real Estate Asia Pacific 2009* survey.

Apartment Residential (Rental) Sector: Some Fall, Others Rise

Ho Chi Minh City, Mumbai, and Bangalore retain their top rankings by buy recommendations from 2008. Cities such as Taipei have risen in rankings based on buy recommendations from 2008, whereas other cities have fallen. For example, Singapore drops from the fifth-ranked city in 2008 with a 52.9 percent buy recommendation to 19th in 2009 with a minimal 11.6 percent buy recommendation.

Markets to Watch

Tokyo

Tokyo continues to be a top-five investment prospect city in 2009, but has managed to move from third, where it has been in the past two years, to first. Overall, the slow yet growing economy of Japan has experienced a severe change in the first half of 2008, attributed mostly to rising food and oil prices. In addition, exports, which often drive the economy, are down due to the overall drop of the global economy. As one interviewee stated, "Tokyo is a weaker market than last year, but clearly stronger than other global financial centers." On the development side, Tokyo is ranked tenth, but as one investor stated, "There is

EXHIBIT 3-13

Leading Asia Pacific Cities

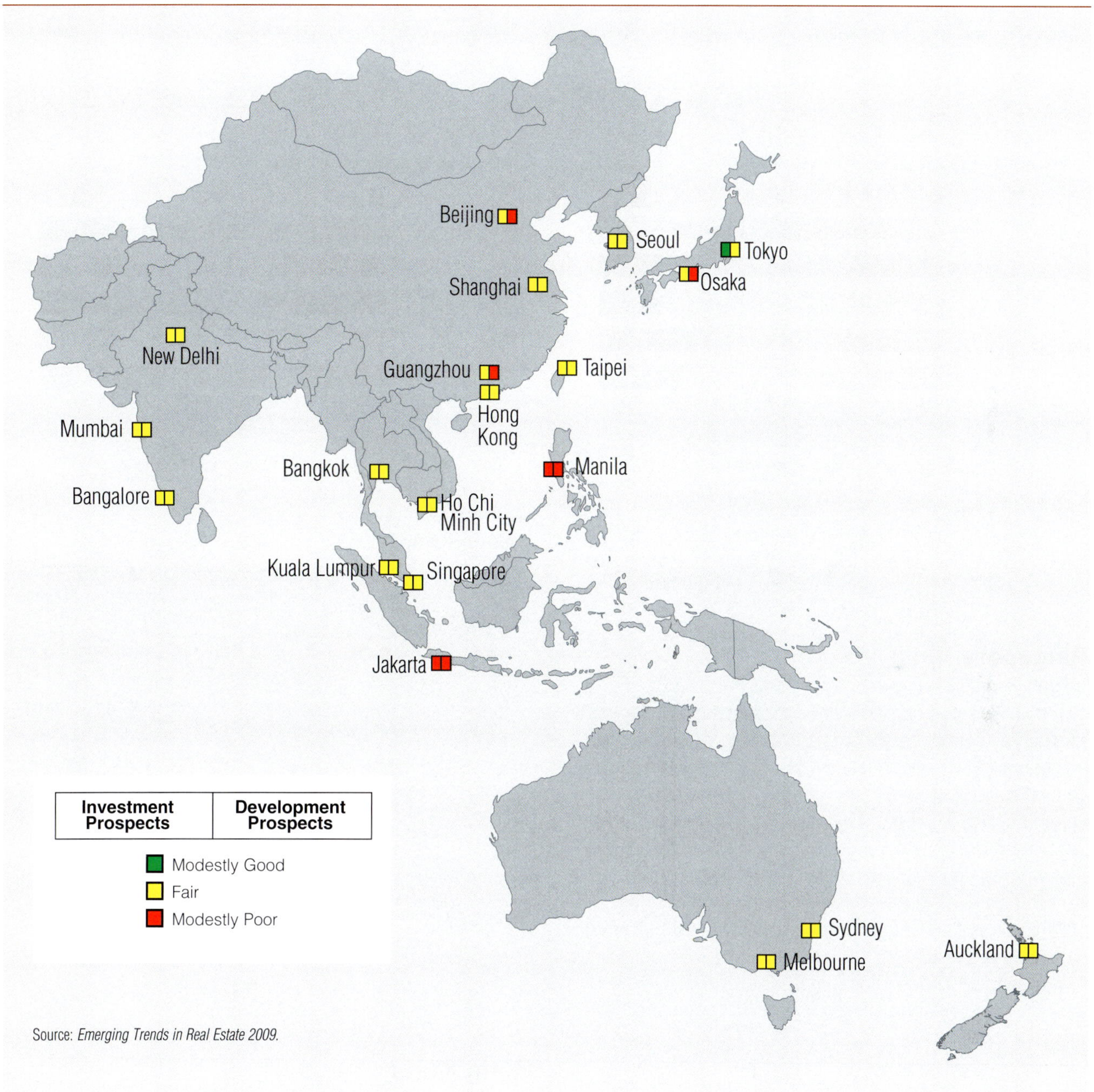

Source: *Emerging Trends in Real Estate 2009.*

EXHIBIT 3-14
Tokyo

2009	Prospects	Rating	Ranking
Investment Prospects	Modestly Good	5.63	1st
Development Prospects	Fair	5.04	9th
Risk	Low	6.65	1st

Investment Recommendation of Survey Respondents

	Buy	Hold	Sell
Office	46.7%	43.3%	10.0%
Retail	25.5%	56.4%	18.2%
Industrial/ Distribution	28.3%	54.7%	17.0%
Apartment Residential (Rental)	32.1%	39.6%	28.3%
Hotels	23.5%	52.9%	23.5%

Source: *Emerging Trends in Real Estate Asia Pacific 2009* survey.

no new office product, but companies are also growing, so there isn't a real new demand." From an investment standpoint, the city is the least risky city to allocate capital, with the best risk rating throughout the Asia Pacific region.

Singapore

Singapore offers a central gateway for the Asia Pacific region, a key attribute, and therefore remains the second-ranked investment prospect in 2009. The city's economy has managed to remain relatively sound through the second quarter of 2008, even in light of today's global concerns. Nonetheless, real estate investments throughout Singapore have softened and key institutional players, now with less capital and a lack of leverage, are nonexistent: investment sales peaked in the third quarter of 2007 at US$12.66 billion compared to only US$1.88 billion in the same quarter of 2008. As one interviewee stated, "Singapore continues to offer increasing supply with less take-up; the market must reconcile itself to slower growth and less demand."

EXHIBIT 3-15
Singapore

2009	Prospects	Rating	Ranking
Investment Prospects	Fair	5.41	2nd
Development Prospects	Fair	5.12	7th
Risk	Low	6.60	2nd

Investment Recommendation of Survey Respondents

	Buy	Hold	Sell
Office	23.5%	54.9%	21.6%
Retail	29.2%	50.0%	20.8%
Industrial/ Distribution	34.8%	52.2%	13.0%
Apartment Residential (Rental)	11.6%	65.1%	23.3%
Hotels	24.4%	65.9%	9.8%

Source: *Emerging Trends in Real Estate Asia Pacific 2009* survey.

EXHIBIT 3-16
Hong Kong

2009	Prospects	Rating	Ranking
Investment Prospects	Fair	5.40	3rd
Development Prospects	Fair	5.13	6th
Risk	Moderately Low	5.83	5th

Investment Recommendation of Survey Respondents

	Buy	Hold	Sell
Office	20.4%	57.4%	22.2%
Retail	31.4%	47.1%	21.6%
Industrial/ Distribution	27.7%	55.3%	17.0%
Apartment Residential (Rental)	26.7%	48.9%	24.4%
Hotels	34.9%	46.5%	18.6%

Source: *Emerging Trends in Real Estate Asia Pacific 2009* survey.

Hong Kong

Hong Kong's international competitiveness continues to draw investors, moving the city up to the third investment prospect spot from fifth in 2008 and 11th in 2007. The real estate markets within Hong Kong have been on a rally for the past five years, but demand is projected to slow down. Others might disagree, though, as the city's development rating places it sixth overall. "Many of the Hong Kong developers are cash heavy, so they are well positioned," states one interviewee. Another interviewee supports that statement, saying, "Local and smaller players in these markets will have difficulty and partnership opportunities could lie ahead." Other issues affecting the Hong Kong markets include a rising cost of living, a decline in export of services, and a drop in private consumption spending. Even with these problems one interviewee claims to be content, stating, "We are still seeing sizable rent increases and quick market absorption of space."

Bangalore

Bangalore is the highest-jumping investment prospect of all Asia Pacific cities in 2009, moving from 12th in 2008 to the fourth spot this year. Just as many other countries have come under significant pressure owing to the U.S. subprime crisis, India is no different. However, even with all of today's global uncertainties, the country's economy has managed to sustain its growth pace. Unfortunately, this pace will be difficult to maintain with rising inflation, increases in crude oil prices, and jumps in the individual's basic needs costs. Regardless, Bangalore seems to have continued growth and ranks the number-one development prospect in 2009. This demand shift seems to be driven by new emerging markets within the city, including the biotech and textile industries, along with the IT arena.

EXHIBIT 3-17
Bangalore

2009	Prospects	Rating	Ranking
Investment Prospects	Fair	5.35	4th
Development Prospects	Fair	5.27	1st
Risk	Moderate	4.72	12th

Investment Recommendation of Survey Respondents

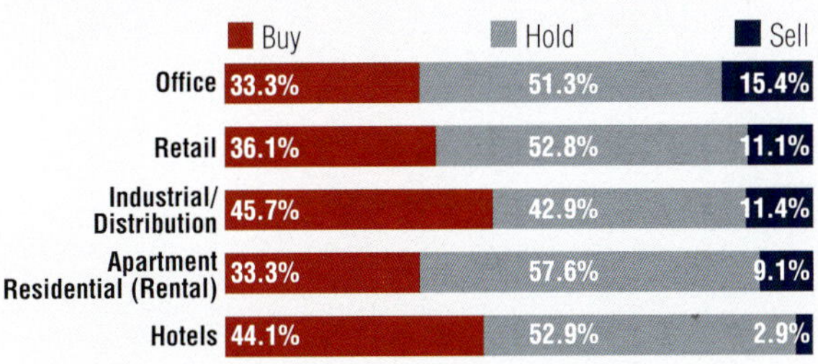

Source: *Emerging Trends in Real Estate Asia Pacific 2009* survey.

EXHIBIT 3-18
Shanghai

2009	Prospects	Rating	Ranking
Investment Prospects	Fair	5.34	5th
Development Prospects	Fair	5.09	8th
Risk	Moderate	4.96	11th

Investment Recommendation of Survey Respondents

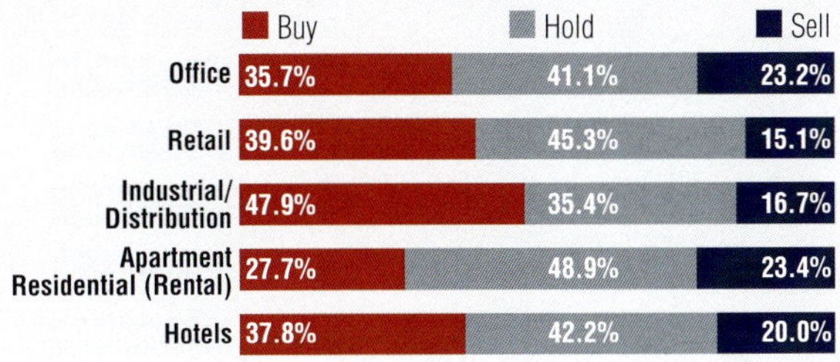

Source: *Emerging Trends in Real Estate Asia Pacific 2009* survey.

Shanghai

Out of the top five investment prospects in 2009, Shanghai is the only city that has had a decline in ranking. In 2008 the city was first, but it has dropped to fifth for the coming year. Opportunities still are available, though, as one interviewee said, "There will continue to be a growing demand for office in Shanghai, but the supply is only increasing at a small pace relative to market size." Vacancies throughout Shanghai seem to be in control, but one interviewee believes that might change: "Rents are projected to rise along with prices." This might have an impact on vacancy rates, but according to the *Emerging Trends* survey there is still room for development as the city ranks eighth overall.

Seoul

The Korean city of Seoul ranks sixth in investment prospects, producing a steady increase in rankings since 2007. In regard to development prospects, the city rounds out the top ten. Korea seems to remain in good economic condition despite the slowdown around the globe. The key economic drivers for Korea are shipbuilding, steel, robotics, wireless broadband, and liquid crystal display. This continued industrial growth will play a large role in keeping

EXHIBIT 3-19
Seoul

2009	Prospects	Rating	Ranking
Investment Prospects	Fair	5.33	6th
Development Prospects	Fair	4.98	10th
Risk	Moderately Low	5.56	9th

Investment Recommendation of Survey Respondents

	Buy	Hold	Sell
Office	33.3%	46.7%	20.0%
Retail	23.8%	52.4%	23.8%
Industrial/ Distribution	21.4%	45.2%	33.3%
Apartment Residential (Rental)	21.6%	45.9%	32.4%
Hotels	18.9%	56.8%	24.3%

Source: *Emerging Trends in Real Estate Asia Pacific 2009* survey.

the real estate market healthy. Many interviewees believed that real estate in Seoul continues to focus on basic fundamentals such as operations and management. One interviewee agrees, stating, "Real estate will survive due to rental growth through these tough times."

Mumbai

Mumbai's lucky number must be seven, jumping that many spots from 2007 to 2008 and now the same to 2009. This seventh-ranked city continues to experience unprecedented growth with its continuing economic development. Key factors contributing to this movement are rising incomes, urban development, and a newfound availability of financing. Unfortunately, these attributes have caused some problems for the real estate markets, as development has happened at a faster pace than the growth of the overall economy. Regardless, *Emerging Trends* survey participants believe that there is still room to develop and have ranked the city third in development prospects. With this growth, though, comes risk and that shows with Mumbai also being ranked the third-riskiest city for investment.

EXHIBIT 3-20
Mumbai

2009	Prospects	Rating	Ranking
Investment Prospects	Fair	5.21	7th
Development Prospects	Fair	5.22	3rd
Risk	Moderately High	4.38	18th

Investment Recommendation of Survey Respondents

	Buy	Hold	Sell
Office	37.2%	46.5%	16.3%
Retail	41.5%	41.5%	17.1%
Industrial/ Distribution	44.7%	34.2%	21.1%
Apartment Residential (Rental)	36.1%	55.6%	8.3%
Hotels	52.6%	42.1%	5.3%

Source: *Emerging Trends in Real Estate Asia Pacific 2009* survey.

EXHIBIT 3-21
Taipei

2009	Prospects	Rating	Ranking
Investment Prospects	Fair	5.20	8th
Development Prospects	Fair	5.15	5th
Risk	Moderately Low	5.66	8th

Investment Recommendation of Survey Respondents

	Buy	Hold	Sell
Office	28.2%	59.0%	12.8%
Retail	18.9%	73.0%	8.1%
Industrial/ Distribution	38.9%	44.4%	16.7%
Apartment Residential (Rental)	29.7%	56.8%	13.5%
Hotels	26.5%	58.8%	14.7%

Source: *Emerging Trends in Real Estate Asia Pacific 2009* survey.

Taipei

With the political cloud now lifted from the city, Taipei has moved back up from a large drop in 2008 into the top ten investment cities for 2009. In addition to investment opportunities, the city provides the fifth-best opportunity for development in the Asia Pacific region. In 2008, the office market looked strong throughout Taipei, with decreasing vacancies and increasing rents. Even though the majority of investors rank office and all other property sectors as holds, there still seems to be a buzz of interest from domestic and foreign institutional investors.

New Delhi

New Delhi's investment prospect ranking moved up to ninth from 13th in 2009. Development looks to be strong for this city as it ranks fourth overall in this area. Survey participants agree that current property investments within New Delhi should remain a hold in 2009; however, 40 percent of the participants believe there are buy opportunities to move capital into the hotel sector in the coming year.

EXHIBIT 3-22

New Dehli

2009	Prospects	Rating	Ranking
Investment Prospects	Fair	5.16	9th
Development Prospects	Fair	5.18	4th
Risk	Moderate	4.50	14th

Investment Recommendation of Survey Respondents

	Buy	Hold	Sell
Office	30.0%	55.0%	15.0%
Retail	27.0%	48.6%	24.3%
Industrial/ Distribution	36.1%	44.4%	19.4%
Apartment Residential (Rental)	26.5%	61.8%	11.8%
Hotels	40.0%	48.6%	11.4%

Source: *Emerging Trends in Real Estate Asia Pacific 2009* survey.

Kuala Lumpur

Rounding out the top ten investment prospects is Kuala Lumpur. The economy in Malaysia has taken hits similar to the rest of the globe, but the city needs to focus mainly on internal inflationary factors that are squeezing profit margins. Regardless, the capital and largest city of Malaysia focuses on tourism as the main economic driver, coming mostly from Russia and the United Kingdom. The tourism dollar is great news for the city and has also been great for the property sectors. This growth gives investors further confidence that Kuala Lumpur is a market they can rely on in the long term.

EXHIBIT 3-23

Kuala Lumpur

2009	Prospects	Rating	Ranking
Investment Prospects	Fair	5.04	10th
Development Prospects	Fair	4.92	11th
Risk	Moderate	5.00	10th

Investment Recommendation of Survey Respondents

	Buy	Hold	Sell
Office	25.0%	54.5%	20.5%
Retail	16.7%	59.5%	23.8%
Industrial/ Distribution	28.2%	46.2%	25.6%
Apartment Residential (Rental)	20.6%	58.8%	20.6%
Hotels	16.7%	61.1%	22.2%

Source: *Emerging Trends in Real Estate Asia Pacific 2009* survey.

EXHIBIT 3-24

Melbourne

2009	Prospects	Rating	Ranking
Investment Prospects	Fair	5.02	11th
Development Prospects	Fair	4.77	13th
Risk	Moderately Low	5.69	7th

Investment Recommendation of Survey Respondents

	Buy	Hold	Sell
Office	20.0%	64.4%	15.6%
Retail	17.5%	67.5%	15.0%
Industrial/ Distribution	23.8%	57.1%	19.0%
Apartment Residential (Rental)	20.5%	61.5%	17.9%
Hotels	13.9%	69.4%	16.7%

Source: *Emerging Trends in Real Estate Asia Pacific 2009* survey.

Melbourne

Melbourne's investment ranking in 2009 is 11th, followed by a development rating of 13th overall. The city isn't considered a risky investment, ranking seventh out of 20; however, the opportunities within this city seem limited. The majority of survey participants rank all five major property sectors as a hold in 2009.

EXHIBIT 3-25

Beijing

2009	Prospects	Rating	Ranking
Investment Prospects	Fair	4.98	12th
Development Prospects	Modestly Poor	4.41	19th
Risk	Moderately High	4.45	16th

Investment Recommendation of Survey Respondents

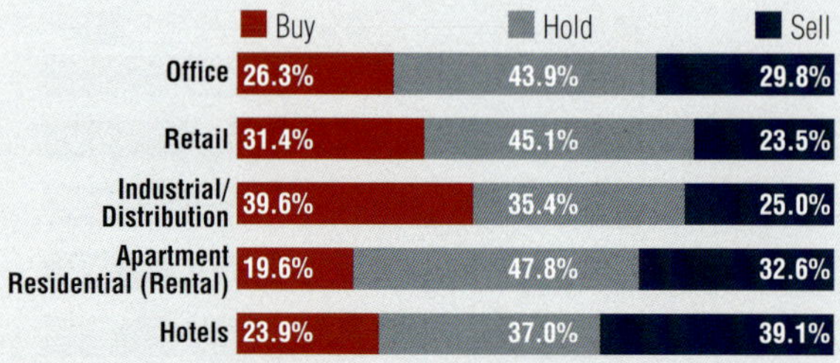

Source: *Emerging Trends in Real Estate Asia Pacific 2009* survey.

EXHIBIT 3-26

Ho Chi Minh City

2009	Prospects	Rating	Ranking
Investment Prospects	Fair	4.92	13th
Development Prospects	Fair	5.25	2nd
Risk	Moderately High	4.49	15th

Investment Recommendation of Survey Respondents

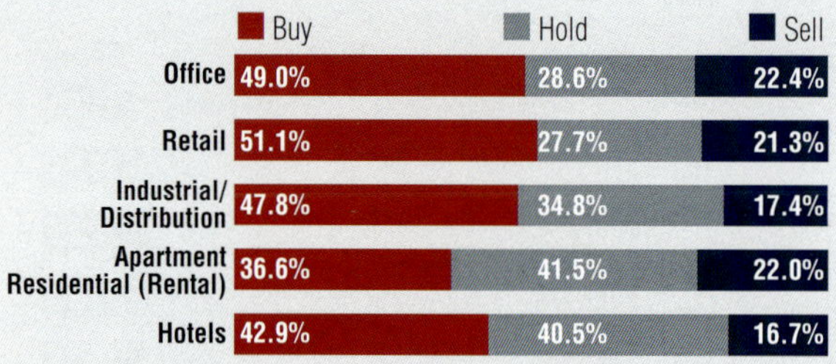

Source: *Emerging Trends in Real Estate Asia Pacific 2009* survey.

Beijing

It is highly possible that the 2008 Olympic hype raised the city's investment prospect to sixth in that same year. However, it is also very possible that post-Olympics it is the reason why it drops to 12th in 2009. Nonetheless, many investors in China enjoy the opportunities there based on the scale of the market and the long-term investment style it offers. A problem, though, that one interviewee states is "there are plenty of opportunities here, but we find them to be difficult markets to enter and exit."

Ho Chi Minh City

Regardless of the drop in investment prospect rankings to 13th, Ho Chi Minh City continues to be an area of interest regarding development, ranking second behind Bangalore. In addition, *Emerging Trends* survey participants believe that it is a buy in the hotel, office, retail, and industrial/distribution sectors. Overall, the city seems to remain on the radar for both investment and development capital.

Sydney

Sydney seems to be taking its real estate growth opportunities one step at a time, moving from 16th in 2007 to 15th in 2008 and now to 14th in 2009. Sydney seems to be in a wait-and-see mode, with all property sectors rated as a hold. "You can't take Sydney off your map for a good sound real estate investment," said one participant. Others obviously agree, rating the city as the third-safest investment.

EXHIBIT 3-27

Sydney

2009	Prospects	Rating	Ranking
Investment Prospects	Fair	4.89	14th
Development Prospects	Fair	4.76	14th
Risk	Moderately Low	6.06	3rd

Investment Recommendation of Survey Respondents

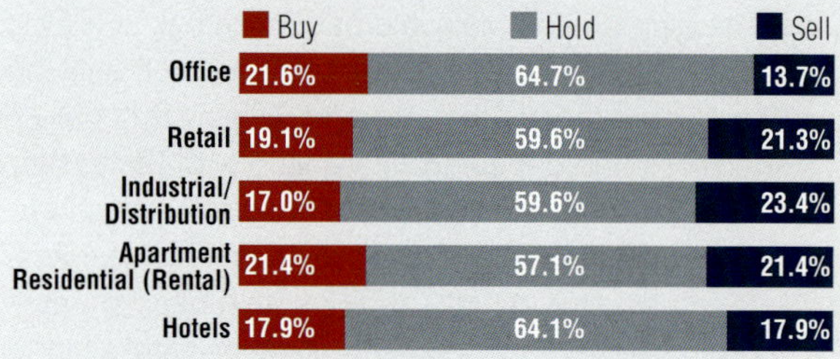

Source: *Emerging Trends in Real Estate Asia Pacific 2009* survey.

Osaka, Japan.

The Rest

The remaining cities all seem to decline in comparison to the 2008 report. The largest drop involved **Osaka**, which has spiraled to the 15th position from fourth last year. As one interviewee stated, "Osaka has a deep market, but one that we just aren't interested in at this time." Development doesn't seem to be an option either in this city, ranking 17th overall. The drop for **Guangzhou** was as sharp, but the fall still places the city 16th for investment, with the same ranking for development prospects. **Auckland** falls three spots to 17th in investment prospects, but survey participants still believe the city is a safer investment, ranking it fourth in risk. **Bangkok**, **Manila**, and **Jakarta** rank 18th, 19th, and 20th, respectively, just as they did in 2008.

EXHIBIT 3-28
Osaka

2009	Prospects	Rating	Ranking
Investment Prospects	Fair	4.84	15th
Development Prospects	Modestly Poor	4.43	18th
Risk	Moderately Low	5.71	6th

Investment Recommendation of Survey Respondents

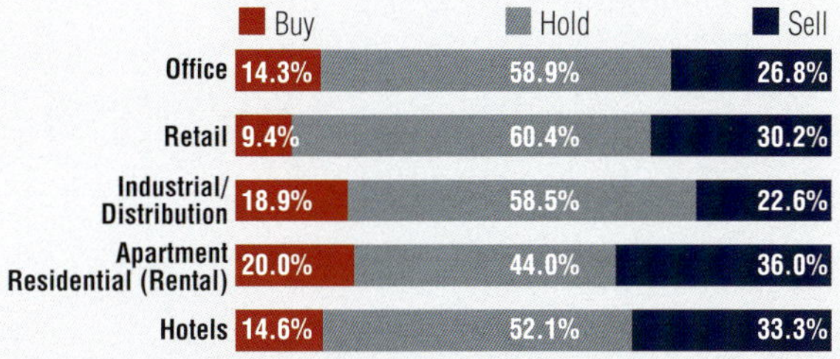

Source: *Emerging Trends in Real Estate Asia Pacific 2009* survey.

EXHIBIT 3-29
Guangzhou

2009	Prospects	Rating	Ranking
Investment Prospects	Fair	4.79	16th
Development Prospects	Modestly Poor	4.47	17th
Risk	Moderately High	4.31	19th

Investment Recommendation of Survey Respondents

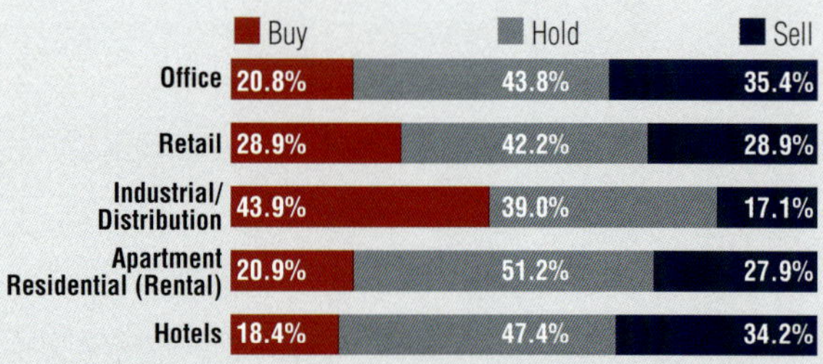

Source: *Emerging Trends in Real Estate Asia Pacific 2009* survey.

EXHIBIT 3-30
Auckland

2009	Prospects	Rating	Ranking
Investment Prospects	Fair	4.72	17th
Development Prospects	Fair	4.79	12th
Risk	Moderately Low	5.84	4th

Investment Recommendation of Survey Respondents

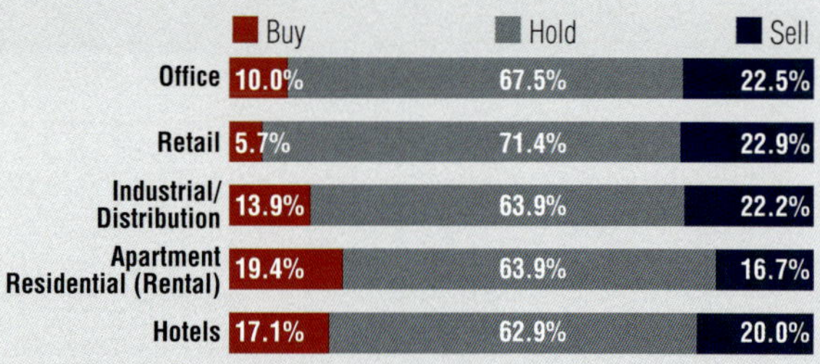

Source: *Emerging Trends in Real Estate Asia Pacific 2009* survey.

EXHIBIT 3-31
Bangkok

2009	Prospects	Rating	Ranking
Investment Prospects	Fair	4.59	18th
Development Prospects	Fair	4.65	15th
Risk	Moderate	4.71	13th

Investment Recommendation of Survey Respondents

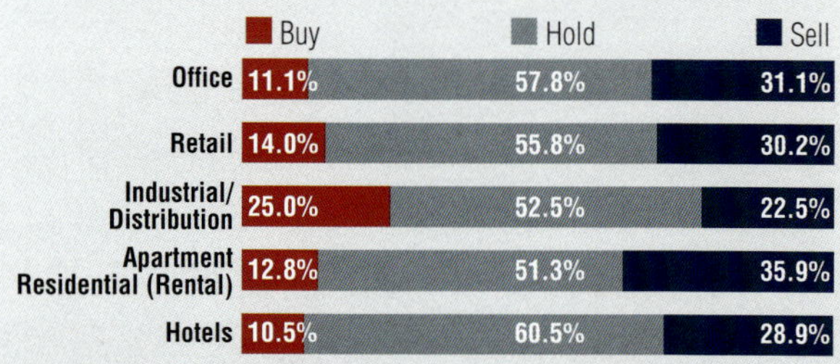

Source: *Emerging Trends in Real Estate Asia Pacific 2009* survey.

EXHIBIT 3-32
Manila

2009	Prospects	Rating	Ranking
Investment Prospects	Modestly Poor	4.32	19th
Development Prospects	Modestly Poor	4.48	16th
Risk	Moderately High	4.42	17th

Investment Recommendation of Survey Respondents

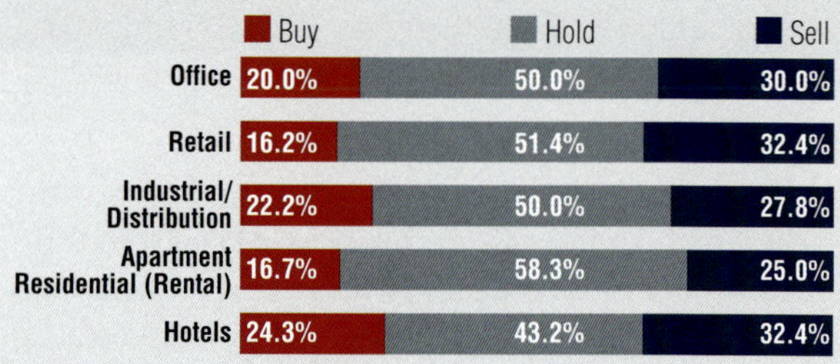

Source: *Emerging Trends in Real Estate Asia Pacific 2009* survey.

EXHIBIT 3-33
Jakarta

2009	Prospects	Rating	Ranking
Investment Prospects	Modestly Poor	4.30	20th
Development Prospects	Modestly Poor	4.32	20th
Risk	Moderately High	3.88	20th

Investment Recommendation of Survey Respondents

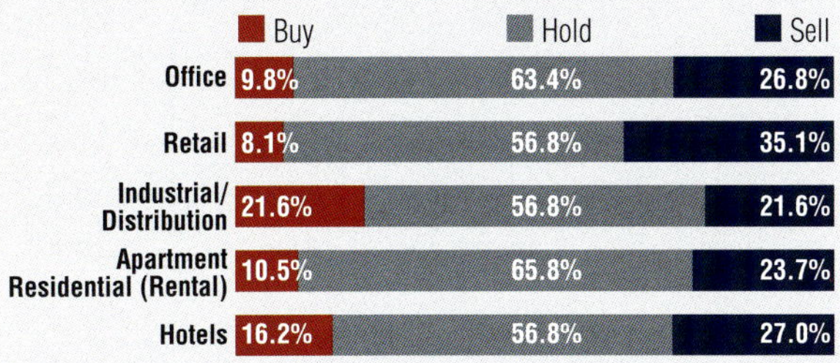

Source: *Emerging Trends in Real Estate Asia Pacific 2009* survey.

Interviewees

Arcapita
Blake Olafson

Ascendas
Chong Siak Ching

Asian Public Real Estate Association
Peter Mitchell

CBRE Research Pacific Region
Kevin Stanley

CB Richard Ellis
Rick Santos
David Simister
Marc Townsend

Challenger Financial Services
Trent Alston

Charter Hall Group
David Southon

Citi Property Investors
David H. Schaefer

Colliers International
David Faulkner
John Kenny

Colony Capital Asia
Grant L. Kelley

Credo Capital Holdings
Costas Papanastasiou

Crispin Property Services
Sam Crispin

CTG Property Holdings
Tyler E. Goodwin

Deutsche Bank
Douglas Smith

DEXUS
Paul Say

DTZ
Lisi Qiu
David Watt

Far East Organization
Philip Ng Chee Tat

Genkai Capital Management
Masatoshi Matsuo

GEO Property Group
Guy Farrands

GE Real Estate
Simon McDonald

Goodman Group
Anthony Rozic

Harvest Capital Partners
Rong Ren

Hongkong Land
Raymond M.J. Chow

ING Real Estate
Hugh Thomson

ING Real Estate Investment Management
Richard T.G. Price
Richard Van den Berg

ING Real Estate Investment Management (Asia)
Kenneth Tsang

ING Real Estate Investment Management (Japan)
Hidetoshi Ono

Jones Lang LaSalle
Andrew Brown

Jones Land LaSalle Hotels
Scott Hetherington

Kenedix REIT Management
Taisuke Miyajima

Keppel Land
Dan Cerf

LaSalle Investment Management
David Edwards
Trent Iliffe

Lend Lease
Ross Taylor

Macquarie Global Property Investors
James E. Quille

Merrill Lynch
David Williams

MGPA
Shigeaki Shigemasa

Mitsubishi Estate
Toshio Nagashima

Mitsui Fudosan
Takayuki Namae

Morgan Stanley
Sonny Kalsi

Morgan Stanley Investment Banking Division
Paul Snushall

Mori Building
Hiroo Mori

New City Asia Partners Fund
Kenneth Fridley

NV Advisory Services Private
Tariq Vaidya

ORIX Real Estate Corporation
Hiroaki Nishina

Premier REIT Advisors
Fumihiro Yasutake

Professional Property Services
Nicholas Brooke

Property Council of Australia
Peter Verwer

Prudential Real Estate Investors
J. Allen Smith

RREEF Alternative Investments
Henry (Wei) Chin

RREEF Asia Pacific
Brian Chinappi
Mark B. Fogle
Tan Yen Keng
Kurt W. Roeloffs

Savills Japan
Christian Mancini

Savills Property Services (Shanghai)
Matt Brailsford

Standard Chartered-Istithmar Real Estate Fund Management
Leslie Chua
Richard A. Johnson

Starr International Company (Asia)
Alison Cooke

Touchstone Capital Securities
Fred Uruma

UBS
Clem Salwin

Valad Property Group
Jeff Locke

Wachovia Bank, National Association
Stephen Au

Sponsoring Organizations

Urban Land Institute

The mission of the Urban Land Institute is to provide leadership in the responsible use of land and in creating and sustaining thriving communities worldwide. ULI is committed to

- Bringing together leaders from across the fields of real estate and land use policy to exchange best practices and serve community needs;
- Fostering collaboration within and beyond ULI's membership through mentoring, dialogue, and problem solving;
- Exploring issues of urbanization, conservation, regeneration, land use, capital formation, and sustainable development;
- Advancing land use policies and design practices that respect the uniqueness of both built and natural environments;
- Sharing knowledge through education, applied research, publishing, and electronic media; and
- Sustaining a diverse global network of local practice and advisory efforts that address current and future challenges.

Established in 1936, the Institute today has more than 40,000 members worldwide, representing the entire spectrum of the land use and development disciplines. ULI relies heavily on the experience of its members. It is through member involvement and information resources that ULI has been able to set standards of excellence in development practice. The Institute has long been recognized as one of the world's most respected and widely quoted sources of objective information on urban planning, growth, and development.

Senior Executives

Richard M. Rosan
President, ULI Worldwide

Cheryl Cummins
President, ULI Americas

William P. Kistler
President, ULI EMEA/India

Rachelle L. Levitt
Executive Vice President, Global Information Group

ULI–the Urban Land Institute
1025 Thomas Jefferson Street, N.W.
Suite 500 West
Washington, D.C. 20007
202-624-7000
www.uli.org

PricewaterhouseCoopers

PricewaterhouseCoopers real estate group assists real estate investment advisers, real estate investment trusts, public and private real estate investors, corporations, and real estate management funds in developing real estate strategies; evaluating acquisitions and dispositions; and appraising and valuing real estate. Its global network of dedicated real estate professionals enables it to assemble for its clients the most qualified and appropriate team of specialists in the areas of capital markets, systems analysis and implementation, research, accounting, and tax.

Global Real Estate Leadership Team

Marc Saluzzi
Global Investment Management & Real Estate Leader
Luxembourg

Kees Hage
Global Real Estate Leader
Luxembourg

Uwe Stoschek
Global & European Real Estate Tax Leader
Berlin, Germany

Asia Pacific Leaders

Robert Grome
Asia Pacific Investment Management & Real Estate Leader
Hong Kong

James Dunning
Asia Pacific Real Estate Assurance Leader
Sydney, Australia

Kwok Kay So
Asia Pacific Real Estate Tax Leader
Hong Kong

European Leaders

John Forbes
European, Middle East & Africa Real Estate Leader
London, United Kingdom

Kees Hage
European Investment Management & Real Estate Assurance Leader
Luxembourg

Jochen Brücken
European Real Estate Advisory Leader
Berlin, Germany

Glen Lonie
Real Estate Leader Central & Eastern Europe and CIS
Prague, Czech Republic

Global Real Estate Leadership Team
(continued)

United Kingdom Leaders

John Hardwick
Real Estate Tax Leader
London, United Kingdom

Sandra Dowling
Real Estate Assurance Leader
London, United Kingdom

Chris J. Lemar
Real Estate Advisory Leader
London, United Kingdom

United States Leaders

Tim Conlon
Real Estate Leader
New York, U.S.A.

Mitch Roschelle
Real Estate Assurance Leader
New York, U.S.A.

Paul Ryan
Real Estate Tax Leader
New York, U.S.A.

www.pwc.com